THE CHALLENGE OF RETIREMENT

Trish Murphy

Disclaimer

This book is designed to increase knowledge, awareness and understanding of issues surrounding retirement. It is not intended to replace the advice that your own doctor or therapist can give you. If you are concerned by any of the issues raised in this book make sure you consult a qualified professional.

Whilst every effort has been made to ensure the accuracy of the information and material contained in this book, nevertheless it is possible that errors or omissions may occur in the content. The author and publishers assume no responsibility for and give no guarantees or warranties concerning the accuracy, completeness or up-to-date nature of the information provided in this book.

THE CHALLENGE OF RETIREMENT

Trish Murphy

ORPEN PRESS

Published by
Orpen Press
Lonsdale House
Avoca Avenue
Blackrock
Co. Dublin
Ireland

e-mail: info@orpenpress.com
www.orpenpress.com

Paperback ISBN 978-1-909895-23-2
ePub ISBN 978-1-909895-24-9
Kindle ISBN 978-1-909895-25-6
PDF ISBN 978-1-909895-26-3

Printed in Dublin by SPRINT-print Ltd.

For Brendan

Acknowledgements

First and foremost, the interviewees deserve the most credit and acknowledgement for the creation of this book. The discussions, coffee and stories were not just informative but delightful and I am honoured to have your trust – thank you.

My colleague Yvonne, herself an author of distinction, was unstintingly upbeat as she read through each chapter on the commute home in the evenings and returned almost immediately with sage comments and corrections.

My friends, against all evidence, continued to believe that the book would be written and spoke about it as a fact – one that eventually I believed too.

My family – parents in their 80s, my twin, sister, younger brother and my own two fabulous offspring – were constantly distracting me with suggestions for entertainment as opposed to hard graft. I'm a sucker for distraction and I enjoyed every minute of not writing!

Brendan – husband, lover and academic – wouldn't let me off the hook and demanded that I reach higher. I hope that the next 30 years will be as interesting and entertaining as the last 30.

About the Author

Trish Murphy is a fully qualified and accredited psycho-therapist, trainer, mediator and consultant working in private practice and business fields. Trish offers counselling and therapy in couples counselling, sexual intimacy therapy and individual psychotherapy.

Having worked in many sectors including criminal justice, third level colleges, schools, the HSE, employee assistance programmes, corporate training and the private therapy sector, Trish has developed collaborative working relationships with a range of institutes and organisations, including Trinity College and, until recently, UCD. She has held a variety of committee positions with the Family Therapy Association of Ireland (FTAI) for a number of years and recently retired from the position of chair. Trish sits on the board of the Irish Council for Psychotherapy and is an inaugural member of the recently formed Irish Association of Sexual Medicine. She has further qualifications in mediation and conflict resolution and is equally comfortable working with groups or individuals.

Trish has a BSocSc from UCC and a CQSW (post-graduate professional qualification) from UCD. She has a MA in Women's Studies from UCD and an MSocSc in Psychotherapy also from UCD. She has additional qualifications in Mediation (Clanwilliam Institute) and Emotional Intelligence (RocheMartin).

About the Author

Trish appears regularly on the radio as a commentator and is a regular contributor to the print media in national newspapers and magazines.

Trish lives with 1,000 college students in a residence in Dublin and has developed great survival skills.

Foreword

Now in my seventy-ninth year, I am not gainfully employed, which is, for me, a heavy burden as I have been a worker since I was seven years old. Right now I feel I am something of a failure because I am not the bread winner in our family. This is not a situation I would have chosen; yet, here I am, somewhat diminished by my circumstances.

Retiring is not something I ever thought of doing or being, perhaps because of some fixed idea. So what could I have to say on the subject? And then I read:

> 'The effect of fear on our intelligence and creativity is particularly bad – it blocks us from seeing clearly and it depletes our natural ability to respond in a crisis.'

Wow! This landed, very much like something I needed to hear. I have spent many moments, too many moments, in not wanting to face my fears – but I've been around a long time. So, thank you Trish for pointing me in the right direction. Life has changed for me, dramatically, and, perhaps because of it, I find myself more willing to open up as much as I possibly can. What I need is what I am and I am told by one whose heart I trust that I am what life needs and what she needs.

I am an optimist in my heart by nature, with work out there on offer to publishers. For years I have used many of the practices Trish has in this book and I can attest to their value. I can also attest to the value of this book. It has opened insights and much needed conversation.

Lee Dunne,
March 2014

Contents

Contents

Contents

Preface

———❧———

'My father had a big job in the public service; he had a big budget to manage and he loved his job and was very identified with it. When he retired, he went from a man who looked like he was ten years younger to a man who looked like he was ten years older than his age. Very quickly he became very depressed and the last years of his life were fairly miserable and the family was miserable because we hadn't a clue how to handle all of this. I was only seventeen at the time and I hated seeing my father going from this strong, accountable, on-top-of-the-game person to someone who was depressed and probably frightened as well, and who had to negotiate his position in the family and that wasn't necessarily going smoothly. So, at the time, I said to myself – probably in my mid-twenties – I want to go into the kind of work that addresses this and I'm going to set up courses for people who are retiring. I haven't done that, but I've set up groups for other types of people and I'm happy to contribute this vignette to Trish's book.' (Colleague, August 2013)

———❧———

It was stories like this that inspired the writing of this book. For the past twenty years I have been running courses and groups in the working world and, since the recession in 2007, many of the interventions have been about redundancy and retirement. Participants on courses spoke of their hopes, concerns and fears and many were pleased that attention was given to relationships, sexuality, mental health and self-care. I also noticed in my psychotherapy practice that I was seeing individuals and couples who were in the early and middle stages of retirement and that the focus of their attention was on not putting up with the way things were but with demanding better lives and relationships and living fully. Families were also seeking help with the new realities of intergenerational living – managing relationships and expectations of adult children and offspring, as well as coping with financial and emotional strain.

This is a book about the psychological and emotional aspects of retirement. Retirement assumes that a person is leaving the world of paid work and so this book is aimed at those people who are leaving that world. Many people were interviewed for this book and gave freely of their time, their honesty and their advice. All hoped that their stories could be of use to others, and their frankness and openness were inspirational. Men and women, single and in relationships, newly retired and long-retired, city- and country-based, all gave of themselves in the hope that others may learn from their experiences and from their mistakes.

As we are all living longer, the messy business of life goes on – as does the need to develop skills and approaches to meet new and difficult challenges. This book pulls together the knowledge I have learned from my years as a psychotherapist, trainer, facilitator, sex therapist and mediator. My colleagues and clients will read their inspiration and wisdom in these pages and I wish to express my humble gratitude to them for the trust, cooperation and faith that have been coming my way for the past twenty years. The people who volunteered to be interviewed for this book were brave souls who took a chance that their stories might prove useful to others. They were sourced through many contacts – friends, colleagues and participants on courses – and all made suggestions as to who they thought might have something valuable to contribute. To a person, they all spoke freely and without restriction. I hope I have done them a good service and I am truly grateful to all of them. Every effort has been made to protect the privacy of the individuals but ages and stories are real and honest.

In order to allow the text to flow, the references are to be found at the back of the book. Particular use is made of the 2011 Irish Longitudinal Study on Aging (TILDA) report.[1] The thoroughness and detail of this study have been invaluable in supporting the issues examined in this book.

The intention is to focus on many of the psychological, relational, sexual and emotional aspects of retirement and stimulate the curiosity and interest of the reader. It is hoped that the reader will be inspired to put many of the suggestions to the test and to perhaps go on to further investigation and experience in his/her area of interest.

Nothing is suggested here that I do not put into practice myself.

Chapter 1

Introduction

There is a new reality to retirement. Previously, people worked hard, were thrifty and were financially responsible, with the idea that a safe future was guaranteed on retirement. There were expectations that retirement would provide time for delights long denied: reading books, visiting museums, long holidays in the sun, tackling the garden, and spending time with grandchildren and friends. Retirement was to be a time to savour the rewards of years of work and planning. The new reality is that this may now be a fantasy and retirement may include lack of money, adult children living at home and negative equity. However, there may be an upside to this – what Marie Murray in her *Irish Times* column calls 'A New Ideology' – one where the focus of retirement is on personal satisfaction and self-development:

> 'A new ideology is emerging. One which says do what you love while you can. Do not save or store but trust in your capacity to have enough if you enact your dreams now. Do what you do best.'[2]

Retirement is a time for reflection, an opportunity for change and development, and a chance to reassess values and principles. Eric Erikson is one of the proposers of a development theory that includes 'Retirement' as one of a number of stages that we go through.[3] He calls it a crisis of 'Ego Identity Vs Despair' and the virtue that comes with successful progress through this stage is wisdom. Growing older is a time when we contemplate our accomplishments and are able to develop integrity if we see ourselves as leading a successful life. However, if we feel we did not accomplish our life goals, we can become dissatisfied and develop despair, often leading to depression and hopelessness. The question is – what are our life goals? Surely they have changed by retirement. Our need for achievement and admiration in the world of work will have abated and perhaps have been replaced with more core values of friendship, love and contentment. If these are true goals then retirement provides the ideal time for development. Having the time to spend on friendships, listen to others and offer the wisdom we have gathered is all possible, and indeed expected, in retirement. We may have to use our sense of fortitude if things are not as we expected, our courage in the face of new trials and our optimism in the face of difficult times. Yet are these not qualities that are worth developing and sharing? Would we not like to be known as strong, brave and outward-looking? As Marie Murray says, 'Do what you do best.'

Retirement is a time of change but it may be different from previous changes we have experienced in that this change may be associated with stopping. This is an error. Human beings do not retire; jobs retire and the person goes on with all the potential they possess. In fact, retirement is only the beginning of lots of changes.

Delia (90) says: 'I am now at another stage of retirement; this time more into my home as I am no longer able to physically move the way I used to in early retirement. I am learning to use the computer so I can order food online. It is a stage of spiritual development and acceptance.'

What has gone before is not necessarily a harbinger for the future. It is better to be open and not stuck in assumptions as they may involve suffering that never happens. Instead of predicting loneliness and difficulty in the future, which can cause immense fear and unhappiness in the present, it is better to enjoy life now and, if difficulties are coming down the road, the time to deal with them is when they happen, not years in advance. Delia could never have predicted that she would learn to be tech-savvy at 90 but she discovered that her 'can do' approach to life continues to work well for her.

Denis (66) says: 'I worked for 40 years and three months and gave the same level of concentration up to 1.30 p.m. on the day I left. Work never cost me a thought afterwards. ... I want to do something about happiness every day. ... Every day should be something special.'

Instead of resisting change, we could develop an attitude of openness to its possibilities. We no longer need to continue achieving and this can be a huge relief. Speaking at the 2012 Relationships Ireland Conference, Charles Handy said, 'When you achieve enough, you are free.'[4] Retirement is a time to let go of achievement, self-improvement and the desire to make an impression. It offers freedom, as Handy suggests, and his is very sound advice to live by.

Death and illness are concerns of later life, yet most of the people interviewed for this book were philosophical about them. Their concerns centred around vulnerability, frailty and the possibility of becoming a burden on others or of needing nursing home care and losing independence.

Aisling (retired 5 years) says that she talks more with her friends about death and illness: 'We laugh about it but you inevitably find yourself doing things – making a will and deciding on issues like cremation.'

She adds that she feels a 'divine presence' and that this offers her freedom and confidence. A focus on spirituality can offer a frame of reference from which to view life and its purpose. In retirement it is inevitable that friends die and a philosophical approach to life, illness and death can develop. It may be a time for people to investigate, discuss and practise an approach to spirituality that is meaningful for them, and it may also be an opportunity to bond with family and friends through these discussions. Death tends to be a taboo subject in our society and yet the people who are closest to it demonstrate fearlessness and acceptance – perhaps it is time to hear more from them about this.

Like most things in life we need some preparation for the next stage of development and the chapters in this book look at these stages from the perspectives of both research and lived experience (specifically, of the interviewees). Chapter 2 looks at wellness and happiness from the viewpoints of physical, mental and emotional well-being. It assumes that if the person is looked after from all of these perspectives then the probability of happiness increases and this is a noble goal for life.

Chapter 3 looks at stress and how to overcome it. This book does not delve into the thorny issues of finances but acknowledges that these issues are of immense importance and that they require professional advice. How we worry about money and how we fear its loss are covered in this chapter. Findings from large surveys such as the 2011 TILDA report on later life reveal that coming from a lower economic background increases risk across the board, from physical illness to mental well-being, and that, therefore, preparing for loss of income and adjusting your lifestyle accordingly is not just recommended but vital. The idea that stress is normal and natural is challenged and a practical focus is put on different ways of overcoming stress and on how to achieve this freedom. The practice of mindfulness is described and an exercise outlined at the end of the chapter.

Relationships are the topic of Chapter 4 and research into what is dangerous and detrimental in relationships is considered here. We also explore ways of strengthening relationships. Same-sex relationships are explored as same-sex couples now reach retirement as openly homosexual people. Chapter 5 looks at sex after 60 and at the particular issues that present for men and women at this time. It is assumed that if you are alive then sex or no sex is a decision to be made, even in your 80s.

Spirituality is the topic of Chapter 6. It is a complex topic as an understanding of what it means must be personal to the individual. Still, those practising spirituality appear to benefit enormously from their practices. Finally, Chapter 7 draws the book to a close and points to further areas for exploration and development; it pays special attention to use of the internet as a resource.

Chapter 2

Wellness and Happiness

The chief aims of life are wellness and happiness. While it is simple to say this, it is far more complicated to delve into it in a meaningful way; to expect wellness and happiness to arrive magically at retirement may be fanciful. However, the good news is that our happiness level reaches its natural peak between the ages of 65 and 75 (at 75 we tend to be as happy as we were at 50), and so there are many naturally occurring factors which can contribute to a growing sense of contentment.[5] Good health appears to be a major contributing factor, as are healthy social connections and meaningful contributions to the world. But there is a caveat – depression is called the hidden trap of retirement so there is a need for awareness and prevention if the possibilities of retirement are to be reaped.

This chapter will look at wellness and happiness from the perspectives of physical, mental and emotional/social aspects. Practices for well-being will be outlined along with awareness and prevention of the pitfalls considered.

The main focus of the book is on the mental, emotional and social aspects of well-being but some attention will also be given to physical well-being as bodies deserve the best care available in order to function for as long as possible.

Mental Health

As Shakespeare put it, 'There is nothing either good or bad, but thinking makes it so.'[6] In retirement there is more time for thinking and if this tends towards the negative then it can be a very lonely and destructive process. For the most part, 90 per cent of the older population rate their emotional health as excellent but a substantial proportion (10 per cent) rate their emotional health as fair or poor. Women tend to report lower levels of poor mental health compared to men but research suggests that depression in late life is both under-recognised and under-treated in both men and women. Anxiety is more common than depression but is also largely untreated: 85 per cent of older Irish adults with objective evidence of anxiety have not been diagnosed.[7]

As most research into depression and anxiety is carried out on young people, the effects of poor mental health on older people are still largely unresearched. What *is* known is that there is a strong link between depression and disability. Nearly two-thirds of older adults with depression have a long-standing illness or disability, compared to one-third of people who are depression-free.[8] Also associated with depression is increased medication use. Of people aged 75 and over with depression, 56 per cent are taking five or more medications; so this is something to be cognisant of. Keeping the amount of medication you take to a minimum and having a GP who is aware of all the treatments are key to good mental and physical health.

Depression is often described as 'the common cold of psychiatry' and it can be characterised by feelings of sadness, loss of energy and lack of interest. It can be experienced as a single episode or as a recurrent experience. It is often associated with anxiety, and the most active emotion, which can take over completely, is fear. Watch out for the following symptoms, especially if they last for more than two weeks:

- Depressed mood
- Irritability
- Loss of interest in hobbies, activities, family, etc.
- Insomnia
- Loss of appetite
- Fatigue
- Poor concentration
- Feelings of worthlessness
- Feelings of futility
- Losing or putting on weight
- Over-reliance on alcohol
- Dependence upon smoking or other drugs
- Loss of interest in sex
- Self-blame
- Lack of confidence
- Getting no pleasure out of life or things that you would usually enjoy

The above symptoms are normal in the sense that we all go through some or all them at some time or other, but if three or more come together and last for a period of time then they all point towards depression. However, the difficulty in retirement is that these symptoms are often attributed to 'normal ageing', vascular disease, dementia or any of a host of other age-associated afflictions. They often go untreated and the person suffers unnecessarily; this can persist for a very long time. It is not acceptable to suffer like this and it often leads to a feeling of being out of control, resulting in poor physical health, stagnation and social isolation. Should three or more of these symptoms persist over a period of time some action will need to be taken. Seeking outside assistance at this point is paramount and there are many options available. A visit to your GP, an accredited counsellor or psychotherapist, a support group, a mindfulness class or an active ageing group, or speaking to family and friends, will all start the process of recovery. Getting help is a sign of liking and caring for yourself and this is the cornerstone of happiness and wellness.

'Anxiety' is a general term for several disorders that cause nervousness, fear, apprehension and worrying. These symptoms can be mild and unsettling or extremely debilitating. Many people suffer from both anxiety and depression and this can lead to suicidal thoughts: 'of older adults with both depression and anxiety, 30 per cent reported suicidal feelings compared to 16 per cent with depression and 5 per cent with anxiety.'[9] Effective recognition and treatment of these disorders is necessary, with particular focus on those living alone or with a disability as they seem to be in the most vulnerable groups. Chapter 3 looks at ways of dealing with negative thinking. The time to implement these practices is when you are well and not when the symptoms of anxiety have already taken over. As always, self-awareness and self-care are the starting points for wellness and happiness and are entirely practical and achievable.

Emotional/Social Well-Being

It is reported that 80 per cent of a person's social life is work-related, which means that when retirement happens only 20 per cent of social life will happen naturally.[10] The rest will require effort, commitment and follow-through. It is not unusual to hear people complain that their relatives, friends or former work colleagues have not phoned or visited; however, the question should be, *have you contacted or organised to meet these people or is time being spent waiting for something to happen?*

> 'Happy people actively seek out other people. They have more positive attitudes to other people, liking and trusting them more. They are open and friendly to people they don't know. In social situations they are more outgoing, warm, gregarious, sociable, lively and energetic. They enjoy social activities more.'[11]

In order to promote happiness, people need to be contributing to society and/or helping others. Happier people tend to volunteer, enjoy helping others and are more likely to donate blood and give to charities. Positive mood increases liking of others and increases your sense of humour, sense of meaning and natural optimism. Happy people do not easily give up, they are not afraid, they do not avoid challenges and their attention tends to be outwards with a focus on others. Taking heed of this, find an outlet that suits your interests and personality and try to get involved in your community. If you enjoy reading, consider volunteering at an adult literacy centre; if you are a sociable person who likes to chat, a charity such as ALONE would benefit from your involvement.

——————

Ian (65) says: 'Being busy is my way of coping. Work had often gotten in the way of what I wanted to do so I now have a passionate involvement in my interests. I feel lucky.'

Sophie (83) agrees: 'A lot of my time is taken up with calling into older people and keeping them company – sometimes I don't feel like it but I always feel better afterwards.'

—◦◦◦—

According to Anna Magee in *Red Magazine*,[12] there are four proven ways to promote contentment:

- *Flow*: Absorption in a single activity – such as gardening, playing with grandkids or cooking – leads to a state of unselfconsciousness and can raise the level of contentment. Multi-tasking and self-absorption increase discontent.
- *Mindfulness*: Observing negative thoughts and letting them come and go, accepting these thoughts as just thoughts, learning breathing techniques and practising meditation all boost mood and increase well-being.
- *Gratitude*: People who focus on being grateful for what they have, rather than focus on what they don't have, are more optimistic. A simple practice is to start every day with an honest, grateful thought – before getting out of bed.
- *Support:* The single biggest contributing factor to emotional well-being is a strong network of family and friends. Being involved in local community and supporting people in your life will benefit you in countless ways.

'The person who delivers meals on wheels and sits and talks with a lonely elderly person, they are giving just as much as anyone … and we receive far more joy than we give.'[13]

An interesting finding on happiness comes from a longitudinal study conducted on Lotto winners and paralysed accident victims.[14] Initially, the happiness levels of the Lotto winners soared, but after a number of months their happiness levels were back to where they started. Accident patients' happiness levels predictably decreased when they became disabled but over time their happiness levels increased above where they were originally and remained there. The supposition is that survivors of accidents value every day as special and focus on the pleasures of life and on their relationships. They value their lives and those around them more and tend to focus on today as opposed to worrying about the future. However, the finding for the Lotto winners demonstrates that while more money initially makes us happier, it seems that once we have enough to live well, a lot more does not make us proportionally happier. Happiness is a very 'now' experience where we operate fully from the present moment.

Cait reports from her hospital bed (where she is ill with cancer): 'A song from post-World War II keeps coming into my head and this was a time of shortages and sadness. It goes "Powder your face with sunshine. Make up your eyes with laughter." Have a laugh and enjoy what makes you happy. Even if you can't walk very far, go for a little walk and appreciate the beauty.'

We can learn much from this research. Focusing our attention outwards and away from our negative thinking is very positive. Helping others keeps us active while learning how to pause and appreciate the moment are all key in our task of making our lives the best they can be. There is no better time to start than now – have fun and do the best you can with what you have.

———◦◦◦———

Dave (retired two years) says: 'I now have more complex involvement with grandchildren. I am more aware of my relationships and also want to support my children's relationships – I don't want to see them as separate. The strangest things become enjoyable – I really enjoy scrubbing the loo.'

———◦◦◦———

Physical Well-Being

We have all been bombarded with information on how to keep ourselves physically well and, while it can appear complicated, it really boils down to three things: good food, physical exercise and good sleep. If we get these things right then the body we have been given will keep going for a long time. But, even though it is simple, it is not easy to implement and we perhaps have a lifetime of poor habits to undo.

Healthy Eating

Research shows us that there are communities around the world that tend to live well until their 90s and beyond and they all tend to have a few things in common. In 2004, Dan Buettner and his team investigated those parts of the world where people live longest and healthiest. They discovered that there are a number of 'hot spots', including the Japanese island of Okinawa, a mountainous region of Sardinia in Italy and the Greek island of Ikaria.[15] What these places have in common is a largely plant-based diet, good fresh air and strong family ties. A Mediterranean diet of lots of green vegetables and herbal teas seems to feature in most examples of longevity. A regular daytime nap is also mentioned – something we tend to feel guilty about in our busy Western world.

We all know that eating local fresh food in season is the way to go but perhaps retirement is a time to indulge in all aspects of food, from shopping to cooking and perhaps growing. Taking the time to shop in local stores for the freshest food can be healthy and stimulating – indulge in the senses of smelling and touching to ascertain the best produce. There is no doubt that eating healthily – even if you are only beginning this at retirement – will have enormous benefits for your health and well-being.

—❖—

Sophie (in her early 80s) is proof of this: 'I was very ill for a number of years and I had to take a lot of medication, but I persisted with healthy eating and taking vitamins and the report I got from my consultant recently was that I had the bloods of a young person – I'm delighted and the proof is that I was out dancing recently until 1 a.m.!'

—❖—

The basics of a healthy diet are well known: eat lots of fruit and vegetables and cut back on fatty meats and processed foods. Salt and sugar should only be eaten in very small doses and drinking lots of water can really improve everything from your skin to your digestion. It is very hard to make big changes to diet but small, regular changes can lead to a shift in patterns. Most people have a resistance to change that they see as difficult, so making the changes interesting will support rather than limit the desired change. Growing your own herbs or vegetables can be very satisfying and these can be done in window boxes as well as in knee-crunching back gardens – tasting your own home-grown food is extremely satisfying and getting involved with local growers (through farmers' markets, for example) can all add to the experience.

—◦◦◦—

Tim (87) has been involved in the distribution of organic vegetables since he retired over twenty years ago: 'It changed my life in many ways. I now have a lot of social contact and conversation about food, recipes and tastes. My diet is great and I've learned to make vegetables interesting and it has kept me strong and healthy – I am out on my bike every day and am rarely sick.'

—◦◦◦—

Alcohol, as always, is a controversial topic and the problem can be that with no deadlines to meet at work there is no incentive to be 'good'. Like most things, moderation is the rule: one to two standard units per day for women and two to three standard units per day for men (visit www.drinkaware.ie for more information on what is a 'standard unit'). It probably takes some time after retirement to figure out what works for you – both the pitfalls and the safe areas. If your own self-awareness is not up to scratch then it is always good to ask a few trusted people what they think about your food and drink intake and take their advice. After all, you asked and they care about you.

Exercise

Making and following a decision about exercise is enormously important in maintaining well-being after retirement. Serious aerobic exercise four days a week can make a huge difference to your quality of life and can be the difference between health and disease. How that exercise is taken is a matter of choice but it is important to also get fresh air and vitamin D. Vitamin D deficiency is common in Ireland and it is thought to play a role in helping calcium absorption and in preventing cancer and, possibly, diabetes. The best way to get vitamin D is through exposure to sunshine but, failing that, taking supplements will help.

Ned says: 'I decided that I would take a 30-minute walk every day no matter what the weather was like. Having a good rain jacket and boots are the only accessories and off I go. The benefit is that the weather never stops me and now people know my routine and so I get to chat and catch up on the local news on my daily walk.'

Not taking exercise will be seen in the future as self-destructive.[16] Exercise is the only way to make our bodies stronger and more supple, and it reduces the risk of age-related illnesses such as osteoporosis, diabetes, high blood pressure (hypertension) and heart disease. It also lowers stress, reduces mental health issues and helps with sleep and relaxation. Even if the weather is bad, gyms and health centres offer programmes for all ages but if this is not on the cards climbing the stairs often and regularly will be a huge benefit. Dancing has many benefits – great exercise, lots of fun and sex appeal – and classes are available in most places. Just attending the local events and 'giving it a whirl' can improve both physical and mental well-being.

Dancing is natural to human beings. Small children dance uninhibitedly and we have many examples from cave drawings of people dancing. It is impossible to dance if you feel self-conscious or uncomfortable. Taking up dancing will therefore challenge the barriers we have to expressing ourselves and that can only be a good thing. It is also social and it connects us to others in a light and wordless way that cheers us up and makes us laugh. Dancing in later life is not about performance, it is about freedom of expression and it works on many levels – physical, emotional, social and spiritual.

If dancing is not for you, find another form of exercise that you enjoy – jogging, swimming, golf, tennis. The key is to find something you enjoy and stick with it. You don't want exercise to feel like a chore; it should be something you look forward to. That way, it will be much easier to form and maintain the exercise habit.

Sleep

As you get older, you can find that your sleep is disturbed and/or you experience difficulty in falling asleep. Any sleep-deprived person knows how quickly their personality can deteriorate in the face of broken or no sleep. A good piece of advice is not to trouble yourself with the amount of sleep you have had – telling yourself to go to sleep now because you will be wrecked tomorrow is unlikely to have the desired effect. Instead, focus on getting up when you wake up. If this is carried out well for a week or so your sleep pattern can regulate and you will find yourself going to bed at a suitable time. Getting up when you wake up means exactly that – immediately. If you stay dozing, even for ten minutes or more, you will feel your energy draining and everything will take even longer. The stress hormone cortisol is at its highest in the mornings and so it is a good idea to move out of bed and dissipate the lethargic energy of stress. If you are particularly sleep-deprived, a trip to a sleep clinic is well advised.

Accidents

Most people stay healthy and well until an accident happens – a fall or a crash perhaps. It is important to accident-proof your home and to establish routines that lead to safety. Having non-slip surfaces in kitchens and bathrooms and installing extra rails on stairs are all insurance measures against an event that can lead to a very long recovery time. Having safety routines can prevent silly but simple accidents from happening – don't wear socks on wooden stairs, sit down when tying your shoes, sit down when taking off a polo-neck sweater, double-check that the handbrake is on in the car, take two trips with the shopping rather than carrying everything in one go, stop when tired, etc. Often people are living long, healthy lives until they break a limb and need care, particularly if they live alone. Such an ordeal can fill them with a sense of vulnerability and fear. As the old saying goes, 'Prevention is better than cure', so safe-proofing life is well worth the hassle.

Medical Care

According to the TILDA report, one in five older adults takes five or more medications. This proportion rises to almost one in two for those aged 75 years and older. There is a significant discrepancy between self-reported disease and objective measure of disease: for example, 58 per cent of men and 49 per cent of women with objective evidence of hypertension are undiagnosed.

All this shows that it is very important to have a good relationship with a physician or healthcare professional from the early days of retirement. Having one person who knows your medical history and who can judge the interaction of all your different medications is crucial when it is common to attend different professionals and indeed different centres for different illnesses. Attending medical checks regularly should be a normal part of retirement and this can lead to early detection of illness and therefore offer the best chance of recovery. However, men traditionally attend their GPs far less frequently than women do and this situation needs to change if they wish to live longer and healthier lives. Also, alternative practitioners can have a role in supporting healthy living with many offering guidance and support for creating change in all aspects of well-being.

Some diseases vary in prevalence between men and women. For example, hypertension, angina and stroke are more common in men while osteoporosis, arthritis and high cholesterol are more common in women. Smoking (one in five older Irish adults is a smoker) continues to be a major risk factor for death from cancer, coronary heart disease and stroke in older age. Consumption of alcohol increases the risk of falls and has been linked to cognitive problems and dementia.[17]

The obvious path to physical well-being is clear and the message has been endlessly repeated – good food in reasonable proportions, fresh air and daily exercise, moderate consumption of alcohol, no smoking, a good relationship with a physician and accident prevention. The difficulty is in implementing the change and the starting point for this is motivation. The motivation should be self-care or, as a familiar advert goes,

'Because you're worth it.' The body you were given is yours to care for and if you think it is worth it you will treat it as if it were the most valuable possession you own – after all, it is. Even the smallest changes, if practised often enough, lead to change – think of the effect of water on stone – and getting support for this will help you get through the difficult times. So, join forces with others and learn to live in a healthy way.

A Holistic Approach

As human beings we need to look after all aspects of ourselves in order to get the most out of life. Focusing on one aspect to the detriment of the others will only produce limited success. We all find it easy to look after some aspects of ourselves while finding development in other areas more difficult. That is the challenge: to be aware of all our needs – mental, emotional, physical and social – and give them equal footing on our to-do list. As Eoin (late 70s) says:

'I am very good at eating well and exercising, but I find it very difficult to phone someone to go out for a drink with or, even worse, to ask out for coffee. I would feel very vulnerable doing this and, while I miss company, this is a step too far. Still, I expect other people to contact me and I'm often waiting for the phone to ring.'

The answers to the above situation are obvious, but having the wherewithal to tackle them is a challenge. The next chapter dissects the causes of the problem and offers practical steps to tackle these issues.

Chapter 3

Stress and Living

There is a common idea that retirement should be free of stress. Many people say that it is terrible that someone is suffering at 'this stage of their lives' or that 'they do not deserve this, having worked so hard all their lives.' However, the facts would seem to contradict these expectations. Retirement is a time when people are faced with many of life's difficulties, ranging from financial to health and loss. Perhaps more than any other time in life, retirement requires resilience, patience, optimism and faith, and if these skills have not been cultivated before this stage then it is never too late to start. After all, Moses was in his 80s when he was asked to lead the Israelites across the Red Sea.

Life up to the stage of retirement may have been very busy: filled with work, commuting, commitments, family and social life. While these activities were demanding, they perhaps did not allow much time for reflection and consideration of where life was heading. When there is a gap in activity (be it work, rearing family, etc.) then change is possible but with this gap comes a sense of dislocation and discomfort, and sometimes we rush to fill the discomfort without allowing it to germinate new possibilities and approaches.

Aisling, who has been retired for five years, describes this past year: 'I observed the whole season of spring through the flowers ... walking in the park every day, a new vista appeared as spring progressed ... imagine that I had never really observed the sheer beauty of nature before.'

There can be a gender difference in responses to retirement. Women often have many breaks in their working life – perhaps for maternity leave, part-time work or taking a career break – and this gives them the knowledge and experience of some of the more stressful effects of not working. Many men, on the other hand, have worked continuously throughout their lives and their experience of not working can be limited to holidays or short periods of sickness. Some men are shocked at the reality of an unstructured life and are unprepared for the loneliness and lack of direction. Many men fill the time with voluntary projects (education, coaching, etc.) and while all this is excellent, sometimes it has the whiff of desperation. It is important to have projects but we also need to accept and reflect on our lives and the need for connection and meaning.

Tom describes the freedom as 'brilliant and scary ... the biggest anchor is gone ... that is my position of power at work. I don't feel respected at home.'

Ian says that he misses 'being used and being helpful. I was a problem solver. The biggest loss is the people – colleagues but even more so the clients.'

There are obviously exceptions to this gender difference. A few of the women interviewed had been single mothers and had worked and struggled all their lives to support their children. Their lives had been fully occupied with the need to provide and any free time was filled by sitting exhausted in front of the TV or going to bed early. As both work and raising children have been completed, these women face a huge challenge in re-constructing a whole life – both home and social – following perhaps 40 years of struggle. Many single or separated women share the same issues as men as they may have had no experience of a break in their working life. However, there is evidence that women are better at social networking than men, which means they may have more resources and support to call on when they retire.

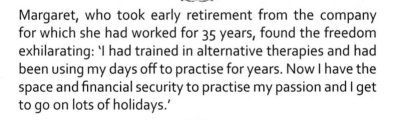

Margaret, who took early retirement from the company for which she had worked for 35 years, found the freedom exhilarating: 'I had trained in alternative therapies and had been using my days off to practise for years. Now I have the space and financial security to practise my passion and I get to go on lots of holidays.'

Stress

Some of the causes of stress in retirement include:

- Lack of finances
- Parents becoming dependent or ill
- Children moving back home or emigrating
- Having responsibility for caring for grandchildren

- Dashed expectations (no money for cruises or holidays)
- Loss of vivacity and energy
- The fear of illness or actual illness
- Loss of a future or fear of the future
- Loss of attractiveness/loss of sexual desire or functioning
- Friends becoming ill or dying
- Loneliness and regret
- Loss of confidence
- Loss of position in society

While some of these issues are serious, many of the causes of stress can be trivial but disturbing.

——◦◦◦◦——

Tim describes an occasion where a young woman offered him her seat on the bus: 'I was horrified when I realised that she thought I was old.'

Frank (late 60s) says that some of the small things become very irritating: 'My wife got upset when she found me sitting on her chair in the mornings, but I liked her chair better than all the others.'

——◦◦◦◦——

Very often, we can rise to meet the really big challenges but allow the small ones to fester and become the source of irritability and annoyance. The practice of allowing the small things (traffic, slow people, supermarket shopping, etc.) to become stressors comes home to roost in retirement as now the time is available to indulge and wallow in the small stuff. Habits of a lifetime may need to be challenged: habitual ways of thinking and behaving that are at the root of much of human suffering.

Stress is so common that we think it is natural. The more we normalise it the more we accept it as part and parcel of life and therefore assume that we have to experience it as part of living. But is this true? Do human beings need to be stressed in order to be effective and function well? Is it possible to approach everything without added stress? Do we not all like to be free of fear, worry and tension, and do we not engage in many things to find this peace? No one is born stressed, yet we pick it up and spend much of our lives trying to find a way back to the child-like quality of natural engagement in life without concerns, self-recrimination and fears.

Retirement can be an excellent time to address these issues. Research into emotional intelligence tells us that our need and capacity to develop emotional intelligence (how to get on with people, etc.) rises naturally until the age of 49 but the upward curve tapers off at this age. Martyn Newman, in his book *Emotional Capitalists: The New Leaders*,[18] suggests that the reason why there is a levelling off of emotional intelligence is perhaps due to a change in life's questions for people in the second part of life – we focus more at this stage of our lives on our legacy, what we are contributing to the world and the meaning of our life's work.

There can be a sense that because we have practised something, such as worrying, for a lifetime there is no point in tackling it now, but in fact when we are in the midst of change we are more amenable to further change and the time can be ripe for challenging our ways and habits. Even if something is practised for five minutes a day, in a year that thing would become substantial and possibly even natural. So, instead of getting better at pessimism we could be practising some freedom. Sitting quietly and focusing on breathing for five or ten minutes a day can release tension and quieten everything in both mind and body. Being able to relax at will is a skill worth having and this is achieved through practice. We choose what we practise and if we practised pausing and sitting still for five minutes every day for a year, we would become excellent at stopping and becoming still. The reality is that many of us are practising worry and anxiety instead.

The Effects of Stress

Before getting to the solution for stress, we first need to look at the effects of stress. We experience them physically, emotionally and mentally (not to mention socially, spiritually and ecologically). The most obvious effect is physical in that our bodies will express stress sometimes before we ourselves know that something is wrong. We may have stomach problems, headaches or sleeping difficulties, sweating, palpitations or tightness of the chest, a tight jaw or tense head and neck, poor skin and many other symptoms. Often our self-awareness is so low that we can experience these symptoms without any sense of their connection to what is going on in our lives.

James's doctor suggested he see a counsellor because of his physical symptoms: blind spots in his eyes, no feeling in his fingers and loss of energy. He asked the counsellor what the problem was – he failed to see the connection between his body's symptoms and the fact that his wife had left him and he had been ousted from their family business.

We often treat the physical symptoms as standalone problems. Alcohol, medication and distraction are all used as an escape from our problems but often become an extra problem on top of the original one. We need to look to the mental and emotional arena to address problematic issues. When the body is suffering from tension you are almost guaranteed that there are troubling thoughts to accompany this physical expression. Mentally, we are rarely quiet and when we are stressed our mental activity can become frenetic. Research from the National Science Foundation[19] suggests that we have up to 40,000 thoughts a day and that more than 90 per cent of these are the same thoughts we had yesterday. Our minds can be very agitated when we are stressed and telling the mind to stop only serves to make the inner thoughts more prominent. Einstein supposedly said that insanity was 'doing the same thing over and over again and expecting different results'. Instead of applying intelligence, knowledge and creativity to a problem we are more likely to react with an already-established set of habitual thoughts and comments, with predictable results.

Distraction/Worrying/Autopilot

Much of our time is spent being distracted, lost in speculation about the future, or in rumination about the past, and this sense of being subject to our thoughts gives rise to much suffering – even if the event never pans out the way we expected. For example, we can fear an event not going well and lose sleep worrying about it for nights beforehand. The worrying depletes us and leaves us less able to deal with difficulties should they arise – it is of absolutely no benefit to us to do this type of worrying.

Our experience is that we are rarely mentally connected to where our bodies are. For example, when driving we are often focused on our destination or engaged in planning. In daily life we forget where we put the keys, ask ourselves if we locked the door, and often have no idea what the person in front of us has just said. The results of this can be shocking.

A traffic warden gave a great example of distraction. He approached a car that was double-parked in a busy business part of the town and challenged the female driver. She was very harassed and said that she had a new baby and just needed to pick up some things from the shop. She then handed the baby to the warden and ran into the shop. The warden watched in stunned amazement as the women ran out of the shop and drove away, leaving him still holding the baby – she returned ten minutes later in a state of distress.

This story demonstrates the problems that a frenetic mind can cause. We have all said things in the heat of the moment only to regret them for a lifetime or we have missed the most important thing going on around us. Being a puppet to a crazy and uncontrolled mind is not the way to peace and harmony. What we need is to be in control of our thinking, or at least be aware that our thinking is getting out of hand. Practising mindfulness techniques, discussed at the end of this chapter, can help you to learn to control your thinking and calm your mind.

Developing a Quiet Mind and Renewing Energy

A quiet mind is what is required to meet life's demands and its pleasures. We need to let go of the inner chatter so that our intelligence can work and we can be fully in charge of our responses. If we are mentally aware we can – or we at least have a better chance of being able to – respond to whatever is happening in that moment and then be free of it. A mind that is always ahead of itself, full of self-criticism or fear of the future, is one that is exhausted and prone to anxiety and burnout.

Studies of energy oscillation suggest a 90-minute circadian rhythm.[20] This means that you need to restore your physical, mental and emotional energy not just every day but every 90 minutes during the day to function well. An effective stress recovery plan that is adaptable to virtually any life is to establish a two-minute recovery drill every hour and a half. Two minutes of mental relaxation will clear the mind and give you a sense of 'being in charge'. For example, you can take a two-minute mental break by closing your eyes, connecting to each of your senses and breathing into any tensions in your body. As you focus on the point of tension by breathing into that spot, you find that you relax. These practices are found in meditation, mindfulness, martial arts and yoga, and there is a growing body of research to suggest the effectiveness of this exercise. To quote Dr Camillus Power, Director of Pain Medicine in Dublin's Tallaght Hospital:

'The physical benefits of stress reduction techniques such as meditation include decreased oxygen consumption, metabolic rate, respiratory rate, catecholamine [a chemical that is released as part of the fight or flight response] release, blood pressure, heart rate, cholesterol, blood lactate and cortisol [stress hormone] and increased melatonin and immune function. The psychological benefits include less anxiety, better pain control, reduced dependency, increased optimism and increased

coping ability, better sleep quality and work effi-
ciency, and improved sensory perception and
better memory.'[21]

If all of these benefits could be found in a pill it would
undoubtedly be a best-seller. Developing the practice of a two-minute relaxation exercise a few times a
day will challenge the idea that stress is a necessary
component of life. However, self-discipline is needed
to create this new habit and so support from family
members and a determination to practise every day is
required. It can take somewhere between 30 and 90
days to break a habit (or more depending on attachment) and therefore consciously practising this short
exercise for up to three months will be required before
it begins to happen naturally.

A detailed description of how to do a short mindfulness exercise can be found at the end of this chapter.

Attitude and Emotions

Attitude and emotions also play their part in the forma-
tion of stress in our lives. Stephen Covey (author of *The
Seven Habits of Highly Effective People*) describes the
90/10 principle of attitude: 10 per cent of life is made
up of what happens and 90 per cent of life is decided by
how we react.[22] Our initial response to something we do
not like is resistance or rejection, and this brings out a
reaction that forms the reality. For example, when we
meet a difficult person we can add frustration, criticism,
anger and impatience to whatever is happening. The
difficult person is likely to respond in kind and so the
experience is one of mutual disrespect and animosity.

Alternatively, we could accept the (10 per cent) fact
that the person is acting in a difficult manner (because

they are being difficult at that moment) and then we can choose our response (the other 90 per cent). We can choose to respond with intelligence, compassion and firmness. If we can accept what is happening then we get the opportunity to adopt a response that fits the situation and not feel that the person or situation is controlling us. Think of the sayings we have: 'He's driving me mad', 'She's making me crazy' or 'He is driving me up the walls.' All of these confirm for us that other people are in charge of how we feel and act. This is not true but much of the suffering we experience is based on the belief that others are making us feel something.

Take our resistance to ageing – is there any point in getting upset at becoming older? Will it change getting older? Will it offer us any hope or optimism? The truth is that ageing is a fact and it is how we react to it that determines the experience. If we accept the process of ageing, we may put actions in place that will enhance the process, such as exercise, nutrition and fun. If we do not accept it, we can suffer negativity and denial and thus lack the preparation that successful ageing requires.

However, it would be foolish to think that habits of a lifetime will give way easily. If we have been worrying, self-doubting or pessimistic for many years, the easy path will always be to divert back to the old way.

Maeve had worked in the restaurant industry for all of her adult life and had resented the servile nature of delivering food. On retirement, she found that she still resented the cooking and serving of food even though now it was only for herself and her husband. Every day, resentment guided cooking and eating and the couple were miserable. When she saw what she was doing she was shocked but she found it slow and hard to let go of the habit of resentment. Maeve used self-awareness and the practice of mindfulness to help her let go of her resentment; the added benefit is that she enjoys her days and her husband more. Mealtimes are now a relaxed, enjoyable experience.

It is necessary to practise awareness, acceptance and discipline if stress is to be tackled. The good news is that even small changes will add up to substantial differences if practised over time. The effect of being stress-free is to feel unburdened and lighter, and this has to be something worth aiming for. More energy will be available for fun, enjoyment and appreciation of life, and even difficult things can be faced with resilience and courage. As one interviewee put it:

'There is more to retirement than me. It's a discovery, and even washing loos has become enjoyable. My idea of being in control has been challenged as I had much more control at work ... but I'm celebrating everything that comes along' (Angela, recently retired).

Fear and Worry

Fear can be particularly pervasive at or after retire-ment. There can be a lot of fear about finances as forces beyond our control come into play. We may also fear illness or infirmity and, very often, our usual methods of dealing with this are practised. Avoidance is probably the most common approach to managing fear – put the thing on the back burner and act like it is never going to happen. As we all know, this approach is particularly unsuccessful as, consequently, we end up shocked and upset when faced with a crisis. We may have no safety net in place or no plans or support system for whatever may happen. The effect of fear on our intelligence and creativity is particularly bad – it blocks us from seeing clearly and it depletes our natural ability to respond in a crisis. Fear can freeze us and the more we practise it the better we get at it – it pervades our relationships, our optimism and our resilience.

What we need is courage and confidence to face our fears. We need to take a step toward reality and calm ourselves. Honesty is probably the most important aspect as it builds confidence in ourselves and elicits support and trust from others.

Many people do not want to own up to the reality of having less money and are reluctant to admit to the new status this might confer. Having been someone who could pay for gifts, meals and outings, it is difficult to adjust to a more restricted lifestyle. Speaking truthfully not only forces a more rapid adjustment (to accepting the reality of retirement) but it also requires courage and challenges the fear of being thought less of. Almost unwittingly, fear can govern our lives and we need to be cognisant of this as fear has such a negative effect on us. Being courageous and speaking up for ourselves is a necessary skill of managing retirement as many public services, financial bodies and medical systems will need to be challenged in order for retirement to be negotiated successfully.

Developing a sense of grace and humility in the face of decreased resources and increased demand is recommended; the upside is that we all want to spend more time with people with these qualities. We need to let go of the fear, be courageous in the face of obstacles and speak honestly about ourselves in order to enter retirement with equanimity and confidence.

The starting point for self-development is always self-awareness – that is, being aware of what is going on in 'me' at any given moment. When we are aware of the mental, emotional or physical state we are in we are in a position to do something about it. Mindfulness is a practice that aids self-awareness.

Mindfulness

The practice of mindfulness is now well known and courses and support groups are available for anyone seeking help. It is a simple yet effective method of tackling stress and becoming more 'present' in one's own life. It can be learned and practised alone or in groups and requires no previous skills or knowledge.

The information on mindfulness presented here is taken from www.cci.health.wa.gov.au, the website of the Centre for Clinical Interventions in Australia, where further material is also available.[23]

Mindfulness is the opposite of automatic pilot. It is about experiencing the world that is firmly in the 'here and now'. It offers a way of freeing oneself from automatic and unhelpful ways of thinking and responding. The principles of mindfulness are set out here and a short practice for letting go is outlined. It is an exercise that can be easily practised.

Benefits of Mindfulness

By learning to be in a mindful mode more often, it is possible to develop a new habit that helps to weaken old, unhelpful and automatic thinking habits. For people with emotional problems, these old habits can involve being overly pre-occupied with thinking about the future, the past, themselves or their emotions in a negative way. Mindfulness training in this case does not aim to immediately control, remove or fix this unpleasant experience. Rather, it aims to develop a skill to place you in a better position to break free or not 'buy into' these unhelpful habits that are causing distress and preventing positive action.

Core Features of Mindfulness

Observing

The first major element of mindfulness involves observing your experience in a manner that is more direct and sensual (sensing mode), rather than being analytical (thinking mode). A natural tendency of the mind is to try to think about something rather than directly experience it. Mindfulness aims to shift one's focus of attention away from thinking to simply observing thoughts, feelings and bodily sensations (touch, sight, sound, smell and taste) with a kind and gentle curiosity.

Describing

This aspect of mindfulness relates to noticing the very fine details of what you are observing. For example, if you are observing an orange, the aim is to describe what it looks like, what its shape is, its colour and its texture. You might place a descriptive name on it, like 'orange', 'smooth' or 'round'. The same process also can be applied to emotions (e.g. 'heavy', 'tense').

Participating Fully

An aim of mindfulness is to allow yourself to consider the whole of your experience, without excluding anything. Try to notice all aspects of whatever task or activity you are doing, and do it with your full care and attention.

Being Non-Judgemental

It is important to adopt an accepting stance towards your experience. A significant reason for prolonged emotional distress relates to attempts to avoid or control your experience. When being more mindful, no attempt is made to evaluate experiences or to say that they are good, bad, right or wrong and no attempt is made to immediately control or avoid the experience. Accepting all of one's experiences is one of the most challenging aspects of mindfulness, and takes time to practise and develop. Bringing a kind and gentle curiosity to one's experience is one way of adopting a non-judgemental stance.

Focusing on One Thing at a Time

When observing your own experience, a certain level of effort is required to focus your attention on only one thing at a time, from moment to moment. It is natural for distracting thoughts to emerge while observing, and there is a tendency to follow and 'chase' these thoughts with more thinking. The art of 'being present' is to develop the skill of noticing when you have drifted away from the observing and sensing mode into thinking mode. When this happens it is not a mistake, but just acknowledge it has happened and then gently return to observing your experience.

How to Become Mindful

Mindfulness is a skill that takes time to develop. It is not easy and like any skill it requires a certain level of effort, time, patience and ongoing practice. Mindfulness can be taught in a number of ways. Meditation is one of the key techniques used in mindfulness training, but not the only technique. Mindfulness courses are available in most localities now. More information about where to find mindfulness courses in your area and how to learn more about mindfulness is available below.

Steps for Letting Go

To begin, it may be best to start by practising with minor concerns before moving onto major worries or negative thoughts.

Sit down in a chair and adopt a relaxed and alert posture. Then ask yourself, 'What am I experiencing right now? What thoughts are around me? What feelings are around me? What body sensations?' Allow yourself to just acknowledge, observe and describe these experiences to yourself without trying to change them or answer your thoughts back. Spend thirty seconds to one minute just doing this.

Now bring your focus of awareness to your breath, focusing on the sensations of your breath as it moves back and forth in your belly. Bind your awareness to the back and forth movements of the sensations in your belly from moment to moment and let go of all thoughts. Maybe say to yourself 'relax' or 'let go' on each outward breath. Spend about thirty seconds to one minute doing this.

Now, expanding your awareness to sensing your whole body breathing, be aware of sensations throughout your body. If there are any strong feelings around, maybe say to yourself, 'Whatever it is, it is OK. Just let me feel it.' Allow yourself to breathe with these feelings, and if your mind wanders to bothersome thoughts just acknowledge and let go of these, focusing back on sensing your breath. Continue doing this for about one minute.

Letting go of your thoughts and fears is central to mind-fulness. You first need to become aware of the thought or feeling and by focusing on breathing instead of giving attention to the thought practise letting it go. You may have to practise this many, many times before the letting go is automatic.

As you get more proficient at this, you might try increasing the length of time you spend on steps two and three.

Mindfulness courses are available in most localities now and information can be sourced from local community centres, many GP offices and health clinics. Individual teachers also advertise in local shops, libraries and so on. A wealth of information is available online at www.padraigomorain.com/the-quite-short-guide-to-mindfulness.html, www.mindfulness.ie and www.mindfulnessireland.org – or type 'mindfulness' into Google. A list of suggested books on mindfulness and awareness is available in the Suggested Further Reading section at the back of this book.

Chapter 4

Relationships After Retirement

There is a well-told joke about relationships after retirement – when a man retires, his wife gets twice the husband and half the salary. Within this is a grain of truth. On retirement, a couple will spend far more time together and whatever issues or habits they have in their relationship will now be magnified. For many couples their preferred way of dealing with difficult topics is avoidance or acquiescence, but this will probably not work when spending so much time together. Very small habits can now be the cause of irritation and annoyance, and previously hidden quirks and ticks can bring the relationship to breaking point.

It can take a long time to adjust to a new pattern together, and resentments and difficulties can become the norm. For a person used to authority in the workplace it can be quite a shock to find that they have to take a secondary role at home. Where one part of the couple is already at home full-time having someone constantly around in their domain can be a huge intrusion and burden.

One couple, who are now in their 80s, replied, in response to a query about how their relationship was after retirement, that, 'things are much the same but more so.' They went on to say that the most important lesson they learned is that they need to have separate interests and activities.

———❦———

If both partners work and one retires, there can be periods of intense isolation for the retired partner and pressure on the returning partner to fill the loneliness gap in the evenings. As couples try to manage all of these strong emotions, their old coping mechanisms can be severely tested and, instead of becoming closer, people can drift into their own separate spheres. In Japan, the divorce rate for retirees is very high and there is a suggestion that this is due to the sudden intimacy following years of separation in business and activities.[24] Couples may have to face some truths and realities about each other that are uncomfortable and sometimes unbearable.

This is often a time when intimacy issues surface as couples now have the time to reflect on their love lives and question what is missing or desirable. More and more older couples are seeking counselling as they strive to become more intimate or to address difficulties in their relationships so do not be afraid to do the same.

———❦———

George and Ann, both retired, struggled with intimacy throughout their 35 years together and sought help as they had separated twice during their time together. Over the course of a year they gradually improved their intimacy and decided to celebrate their closeness by each getting small tattoos – this would be a sign of permanence and of a frivolity that had been missing in their relationship until then.

———❦———

An interesting statistic shows that couples who know each other more than twenty years score lower on 'knowledge of the other' scales than those couples who are together less than three years.[25] The proposition is that people in long-term relationships do not like to disturb the peace and instead of saying that they, for example, don't like the dinner, they opt for the anything-for-the-sake-of-peace option rather than speaking the truth. Fear of offending the other person can take precedence over honesty, and knowledge of each other can suffer as a result.

In the 1980s and 1990s, John Gottman and his colleagues conducted studies of couples that were able to predict with 90 per cent accuracy who would stay together and who would separate.[26] They studied 3,000 couples and were able to establish the four things (described below) that a couple engaged in that would almost certainly lead to separation. The theory of 'depositing in the bank' of the relationship was developed from Gottman's studies: this is where the couple puts positive deposits into the bank of their relationship so that when they withdraw (through fighting or arguing) there is enough in the bank to handle the withdrawal. This means that a couple should constantly be aware of the need to 'deposit', through affection, good memories and good thoughts about their partner, positive things into their relationship bank. Many people speak well of their partner to other people but never express these things to each other so, to remedy this, you should implement the practice of 'never letting a good thought go unheard'.

How to Argue

Gottman and his colleagues discovered that, though most couples fight, this does not determine whether they will stay together or not. People fight because they care and it matters that the other person hears their opinion. Their research found that 69 per cent of arguments that couples engaged in were never resolved. Just think of the average parents – do they not always appear to be repeating the same argument, sometimes for years and years.

What matters is *how* couples fight. There is a contention that if couples never fight or argue their intimacy suffers as arguing and making up can be the most intimate thing couples do. If you do not care about someone or something it will be difficult to summon up the energy to argue or to pursue the argument. However, habits and history play a big part in this. A couple usually has developed a particular way of arguing and this can be destructive, e.g. one person attacks or nags and the other goes silent or disengages.

———

Michelle and John were married for twenty years and had developed a method of arguing that was particularly destructive. Michelle would stand up, fists threatening, and demand to be listened to while John would stretch out on the chair, hands behind his head – the embodiment of relaxation. John's response raised the level of conflict to a new level.

———

Couples develop a habit or a pattern of arguing or fighting early in their relationships and like most habits these can be particularly hard to break. For example, some couples fight in a very passive way and an outsider might be hard-pressed to notice the nuances going on underneath the civilised exterior. What is important is that you look at your method of arguing and see if this needs to be changed. If even one person changes how they argue, the outcome can be completely different.

Practical Advice on How to Argue Better

- Ground yourself: pause and breathe, and remember your aim is to be heard and understood
- Start with a question to lessen the aggression, e.g. 'Are you up for a difficult discussion?'
- Own your own feelings: 'I'm feeling very strong about this issue and so I might come across as angry.'
- Remember the relationship: 'I'm always going to have your back and this issue will not change that.'
- Humour: a light, optimistic approach will go a long way towards helping you to be understood.
- Listen: if your partner feels understood, there is a far greater chance they will be interested in hearing your side of things.

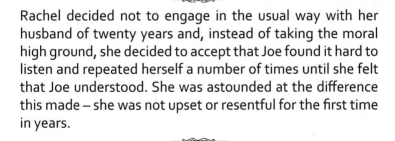

Rachel decided not to engage in the usual way with her husband of twenty years and, instead of taking the moral high ground, she decided to accept that Joe found it hard to listen and repeated herself a number of times until she felt that Joe understood. She was astounded at the difference this made – she was not upset or resentful for the first time in years.

The most common arguments in relationships tend to be around in-laws, money, sex, housework and how to spend mutual time together. Many people repeat the same argument for years with little variation and few understand that the positions they adopt can some-times come from their own family of origin and not their current relationship. For example, if your father or mother had many affairs, it may be that in your own relationship you are hyper-vigilant, insecure and constantly demanding re-assurance. Try as you might, you may never achieve resolution in your current relationship unless you address your childhood insecurities and experiences.

Many people have had affairs but, because of the difficulty in getting reliable statistics for an activity many people do not want to admit to and the fact that different people have different definitions of what constitutes 'cheating', we cannot be sure how prevalent affairs actually are. However, one widely quoted study suggests that as many as 60 per cent of men and 40 per cent of women have had an affair.[27] Perhaps the world of work provided a distraction from these memories but on retirement people can find that their sense of forgiveness or forgetfulness is not quite complete and that there are left-over feelings of anger and fear. Often, there are secrets from the past, such as abortions or adoptions, and retirement is often a time when a couple's relationship is threatened by such revelations. Instead of the ease with which many people expect to enter relationships at retirement, many couples experience frustration, impatience, intolerance and fear.

Phyllis was contacted by the daughter she had given up for adoption when she was eighteen. She had never told her husband of this and her own children and grandchildren had no idea of this secret. Although she decided not to meet her daughter, her grief and fear put up a huge emotional barrier between herself and her husband, and he could not understand her distance and tears.

The time when adult children leave home can also be one of loneliness and loss, and each partner will have their own method of coping. It is easy to resent your partner's apparent 'unfeelingness' if you are suffering and often your emotions get deflected as anger at your partner. The opposite can also cause problems, when adult children return to live at home and their parents have adjusted well to having their own lifestyles and comfort – not to mention the financial cost of more people living in the house. Very often, adult children quickly return to behaviour more reminiscent of child-hood, expecting their parents to provide food, washing, and so on. Parents do not want to cause financially strapped children more distress and so they suppress their feelings of being taken for granted. The result can be explosive arguments or flare-ups.

However, what really bonds us as human beings is adversity: arguing, compromising and making up is the most intimate thing a couple can do. If we stay in our comfort zones no development happens and, to quote an old saying, 'the test of a man is not what he has achieved, it is what he has overcome.' It is never too late to achieve freedom from fear, impatience or the past, and perhaps retirement is a time when this freedom becomes a reality.

Most couples struggle through the difficulties of relationships without benefiting from the knowledge and research that are available. This means that much unnecessary suffering can happen even though the answers are readily available. Some of the more common pitfalls are outlined below and the issues that spell the most disastrous aspects in relationships follow later in the chapter. While the way out of diffi-culties may seem obvious, it is having the presence of mind and the determination to put these into practice that will make the difference to any relationship.

Globalisation

Starting a sentence with, 'You always ...' or 'You never ...' will always result in the opposite to what you want. If you want your partner to sort out the bills and you start your conversation with 'You never take responsibility for the bills', they are unlikely to jump up and ask how they can help you. The term 'globalisation' applies to this activity in which we attack the other person from a universal perspective – we can take responsibility for one mistake or a couple of mistakes but we will resist taking the blame for everything. If you want someone to change their behaviour, wait until you have their attention, have faith in their capacity and ask them firmly to do it. This has the best chance of succeeding.

Taking Offence

Taking things personally is also a familiar problem. The language is important here. You have to 'take' offence as, if you choose not to, it won't happen: nobody can make you feel anything without your consent. If your partner is having a bad day and they take it out on you, you do not have to become upset or angry. It is possible to let the bad mood stay with them and not join it. The old saying comes to mind: 'Resentment is like taking poison and expecting the other person to die.' No one can make you mad, crazy or drive you up the walls without your consent. Knowing this is a key to freedom. Remember the 90/10 principle.

Blaming

Blaming is commonly thought of as the biggest issue in couple conflict but Gottman's research finds that while it causes difficulties, blaming is not the most destructive activity in a relationship. Nagging can be very wearing but at least it displays an interest in the relationship. It seems that women do 80 per cent of the complaining and that the most successful relationships are those where the husband listens and adjusts his behaviour. Research over the years suggests that, in order to be happy, men just need to be married but women need to have good-quality relationships. Thus, women strive to better the partnership. However, nagging can result in the other person retreating into silence, or rolling their eyes, and this can become a pattern in which neither partner's position is heard.

Cross-complaining is also an issue. This is where one issue is being tackled and other issues are tacked on to it – for example, 'You never do the dishes anymore – and you were disrespectful to my parents last week.' Again, it is very unlikely that the person in receipt of this will rush to do the dishes and perhaps their only motivation might be 'anything for a quiet life'.

Holding on to the Past

Bringing up all of the issues from their shared past can cause a lot of friction in a couple's relationship. If you do not let go of the past then the suffering that happened when your partner ignored you or let you down is dragged into the present. Often we hold on to these resentments out of fear that our partner might repeat the mistake and we don't want to be made a fool of. However, the effect of holding on to fear and the past is utter lack of freedom in the present. No relationship needs to be guided by fear and it is up to each person to take responsibility for their actions. In other words, if you forgave an action then follow that forgiveness, and if you regret an action learn from it and do not repeat it.

The Four Things that Signal Disaster in a Relationship

While the above mentioned aspects of relationships all cause problems, Gottman found that it is the next four that signal the end if they are practised frequently and without the antidote of affection and humour.

Contempt

Contempt is always described as the most destructive attitude in any relationship. It can be recognised as any response, physical or verbal, that puts the other person down – for example, when a person throws their eyes up to heaven when their partner speaks or replies sarcastically to a comment from their partner. Belligerence is also destructive as people dig their heels in and will not respond to reason. Partners can be quite subversive in their resistance, as the old Ethiopian proverb says: 'When the great lord passes, the peasant bows deeply and silently farts.' These responses should come with a warning as research is consistent in deeming contempt and belligerence as two of the major factors that will lead to separation.

Stonewalling

Gottman used the term 'stonewalling' to describe the second problem in relationships. By this he meant shutting one's partner out by retreating behind an emotional stone wall – the body is there but the mind and emotions are somewhere else. It means that the relationship cannot progress, as it is impossible to have a relationship with just one person participating. Usually, stonewalling is characterised by a feeling of being overwhelmed and it can be categorised as a defensive mechanism. However, if this becomes a pattern then the relationship is almost certainly doomed.

Criticism

Criticism is the most divisive factor in any relationship (work or home) and it can be described as any thought or action that gives the message to a person that they are deficient, useless, washed-up or a waste of space. The difference with constructive criticism is one worth making. When you have faith in your partner's potential and you know they can do better, then it is possible to challenge them or push them and your presence can be a strong positive influence. However, if you challenge them with the conviction that they are inept or useless, your influence will be unstintingly bad. For example, I could challenge my partner's relationship with his family by saying, 'I know you can do better that that and it is not worthy of you to act so dismissively.' This same message could be delivered destructively by saying, 'You are such a negative person' or by saying nothing and acting disappointed. The effects of criticism are intimidation and isolation – signalling the end of any decent relationship.

Defensiveness

Finally, it is not blaming but defensiveness that causes the biggest rift in relationships. When we are defensive, we focus all of our energy and attention on ourselves and on how right we are – leaving no energy for hearing or understanding our partner. Usually what happens is that one person makes a complaint and the other person retreats, leading to a more vociferous voicing of the complaint and further retreat, etc. A merry dance ensues until each partner is convinced of the other's indifference or badness. An added problem can be a righteous code of behaviour in the home. Sometimes it can feel like walking on eggshells – trying to decipher whether it is safe to relax or whether something is expected that, if not discovered, could lead to a distant or difficult evening. For example, you come home in the evening and have to check the mood of your partner before risking tossing your coat or bag on the floor, resulting in your partner blowing up. This can set up a type of 'parenting' relationship rather than one of equals.

The Effect of Negativity on Relationships and How to Combat It

A study of 700 couples in 2002 confirmed Gottman's work, with its authors claiming that they too could predict divorce with over 90 per cent accuracy.[28] Partners who showed affection, humour and happiness got maximum points and those who showed contempt or belligerence got minimum points. They discovered that if either spouse was constantly negative then divorce was inevitable and that those who viewed marriage as being mainly about companionship enjoyed the most stable relationships.

Both studies suggest a five-to-one ratio between positive and negative engagements in successful relationships, and this ratio also features in Maureen Gaffney's book *Flourishing*.[29] That is, where any of the four negative responses are present then a couple needs five times more joy, humour and affection to combat the presence of the negative aspects.

Each partner needs to take responsibility for their own positions, actions and feelings. Once it is recognised that each person is in charge of their own happiness (not their partner's happiness) then it is possible to develop and practise good fighting skills such as humour, tolerance and authenticity. Learning to use questions rather that accusations can defuse a potential situation, as can remembering that the strongest person at any given moment is the one with the most self-awareness and self-control. Questions focus the attention away from self-talk and criticism and on to your partner, thus defusing the situation and opening up communication. Some helpful questions are:

- Do you think there is a better way/time to have this conversation?
- If we were in a really good place, how do you think we might deal with this situation?
- Do you need to talk about this or would you like some help with this situation? Know that I'm always available for you or I will support you talking to someone else if you'd like.

Another suggestion is to watch for the rise of emotion when arguing, walk away for twenty minutes and then return to the fray. When you return, you will have full use of your faculties, because you have calmed down, and the argument or disagreement can be tackled with reason and openness.

Medically, the group with the longest longevity are those who are married.[30] Research conducted over seven years shows that married couples have mortality rates 10–15 per cent below the population as a whole. The researchers' hypothesis is that well-adjusted individuals are more likely to establish long-term relationships, a view that is supported by another study.[31] The findings of this study are that the capacity for romantic love owes much to each individual's own personality strengths and that those who are long-term married tend to be confident and have high self-esteem. They value their partner and want to be with them but they are not jealous or possessive. Therefore, being in a successful relationship requires that a person has continuous self-development and is evolving as a human being. Commitment is also linked to higher living standards and associated with networks of support that contribute to overall happiness and success in life.

To have a successful relationship means that you are likely to live longer, be more developed as a human being and have higher confidence and less loneliness. All this makes being in relationship worthwhile and the icing on the cake is that you are happier, lighter and more engaged with life.

Confidence is being happy being who you are regardless of who you are with, where you are or what you are doing. It means having faith in yourself that you will respond to whatever you have to face no matter how difficult that is. If you fear that your partner will leave you, you must have faith in your ability to recognise that they are withdrawing and also in your ability to survive if they chose to leave. Holding on tight to someone usually has the effect of them pulling away. Instead, offer them (silently) the freedom to stay with you or not as they choose; that is an act of love.

Housework

The latest figures from the London School of Economics[32] show that single women put seven hours a week into housework, while wives and cohabiting girlfriends do more than twelve hours every week. Men (whether single or in a relationship) do just four to five hours. However, the good news is that the report also shows that men who do more housework have more intimacy. Many couples have arguments about housework – often these intensify on retirement – and there is a danger that the relationship can become focused on small things. The principle of 'you become what you practise' should be noted here. If a couple practises bickering, pettiness and resentments then these are exactly what grow in the relationship.

A strong, healthy man taking early retirement and his wife were considering what do about division of labour in the house now that he had retired. He said, 'I do not want to encroach on my wife's domain and interfere with the running of the house.' His wife was not sure about this but could see the merit in his argument. However, when the husband was asked whether their young adult children, who lived at home, needed to do their share of the housework, he was very clear in demanding that they do their share and that it was unfair to expect their mother to do all of their washing, cooking and cleaning. It then dawned on him that perhaps the same argument applied to him too (participant on retirement course, 2012).

When one person in a relationship feels that the other is not doing their share, they can feel undervalued and somewhat abused. This is why the argument of who cleans the bathroom is so common and so impor-tant – the person we need to feel most valued by is our partner. What is important is that both people feel that their contribution to the relationship is valued.

Achieving that balance will be unique to each relationship. For example, it might happen that one person deals with all the bills and finances and the other deals with the shopping and cooking. What matters is that the conversation about each person's contribution to the relationship is ongoing in the face of changing circumstances.

How to be listened to about the equality-of-housework argument is an important aspect of this. Appeal to your partner's sense of justice and their commitment to your relationship and then help them to follow through on their task. The worst scenario is if you demand your partner makes a contribution and then you criticise it for not being good enough; it is unlikely that your partner will be encouraged to help out again in this scenario. Firmness, belief in your partner and an open and supportive approach have the best chance of working.

Creating a Positive Relationship

Every couple needs more fun, light-heartedness, openness and engagement. Reminding each other of what you want the relationship to become is one way of achieving this and having memories of good times can act as a motivator. Photographs, music, movies and clothing can all play their part in supporting the positive aspects of a relationship. Paying attention to what already works in the relationship will give it strength and durability while focusing on negativity will put a strain on a couple in the long term.

All couples need to practise courage to face what life may throw at them and practising faith in each other will make both the individuals and the relationship strong and resilient. Having the courage to challenge habits and patterns will benefit your relationship, even if it can feel daunting at the time. Suspending judgement and criticism is the essence of depositing good stuff in the bank. It is never too late to work on a relationship or to seek happiness. As Stephen Covey says:

'... the most important work you'll ever do is ahead of you, never behind you, therefore, never retire from making meaningful contributions to society. The key to life is not accumulation. It's contribution.'[33]

Complicated Family Relationships

Sometimes those at retirement stage are sandwiched – elderly parents need looking after or adult children are returning home due to financial pressure. Your expectations of freedom and peace can be crushed and ideas of travel and comfort might have to be jettisoned in the face of the needs of others. Relationships can crash and burn in the face of such pressure – indeed previously good parent–child relationships can be put under enormous strain as everybody feels hard done by. As financial pressures mount, expectations and plans for an easy future have to be re-addressed and coped with. This is where all of the skills learned in one's own relationship come to the fore: patience, tolerance, courage and forbearance are all necessary here. However, in spite of practising good self-management, sometimes outside help is required to address issues and patterns that may have their roots in childhood. Even one session with a family therapist or mediator can help establish new rules and allow the unspoken into the open; it may be the best hour spent by the new extended family.

—❦—

'Myself and my wife were enjoying the new freedom of a house to ourselves – though of course we missed our children. We had planned to put in a new kitchen and perhaps do some travelling. But the recession has brought our children home with their families and we are now supporting them again so all our plans are on hold. My wife and I can see this situation going on into the future but we would never say anything for fear of causing even more pain and hardship for our children' (Bill, 64).

—❦—

Being a Carer

When you are caring for older people, support networks are essential. You can go from working full time, with all of the associated social supports, to almost full-time caring with little social contact. Depression and loneliness can ensue, so at all times remember the air stewards' instruction: always put on your own mask first, before attending to other people. It is only when you, the carer, are well looked after – physically, emotionally and socially – that you are in a position to look after others. If not, then you may be presenting an image of martyrdom or sacrifice that those being cared for may not appreciate. Many support groups exist for carers; all it takes is the initial phone call or email to initiate support. Traditionally, men have been more reluctant than women to engage in community supports but with the decline of pub culture it is probably more necessary than ever for men to find solutions to isolation.

'I find that caring for my mother is a 24-hour job. Even if someone else in the family is with her, I have to organise and oversee it. My own children complain that I am never free to do things with them and I feel permanently guilty. I often find my mind going to the time after she dies and it makes me feel like a bad person for thinking this way as I love her. The strain can be terrible though, and I can feel very resentful of my siblings for not doing their share' (Anne, 54 and a single parent).

Call a family meeting and get a friend or professional to chair it. This will offer the best chance of coming to a more equitable approach to the care of the elderly. The problem is that this new arrangement can last for a while but then slip back into the old ways after a couple of weeks or months. Therefore I suggest that a number of family meetings are arranged over a period of several months to review how things are going. These meetings should be arranged by someone other than the primary carer as they will feel even more burdened if it is left to them.

Support organisations for carers are listed in the Useful Resources section at the end of this book.

Initiating Relationships After Retirement

For separated or widowed people, it can be a struggle to expose oneself to a relationship again but often when energy returns after the grief of bereavement or separation so does the desire to engage meaningfully with another person and companionship can be the goal.

Ruth retired from teaching, having divorced five years previously. She was interested in a relationship and eventually found the courage to ask out a male neighbour. They had a lovely night but he declined a second date. Instead of sinking into embarrassment, Ruth felt emboldened by her risk in asking someone out and decided to do so again.

Like Ruth, many people are interested in a relationship but are either too fearful or lazy, or simply do not know where to start in seeking one. There is no doubt that if we continue with the same behaviour and social activities the same outcomes will result. Most people need to get out of their comfort zone if they are to initiate new relationships, but doing this requires courage and enthusiasm. Many people are embarrassed by their desire for a relationship and feel that they should be 'done with that' at their age but, as John (75) says, 'My girlfriend moved in with me four years ago and moved out two years ago but I'm still hopeful.' He adds that, while he is hopeful for the relationship in question, he is still open to other offers and often meets other women. He does not see age as a barrier. Finding people to date requires energy and focus. There are many ways to do this, such as joining social groups or clubs, saying yes to social events and, perhaps, joining a dating agency. Rejection is still part of the dating game but at least there is a feeling of being alive and with feeling alive comes desire and attraction.

Same-Sex Relationships

Same-sex couples are now reaching retirement age at a time when they can be open about their relationships, but they still face significant difficulties. Even for those who are in a civil partnership, parts of their lives may have to be lived in secret. Tanya (recently retired from the civil service) reports that when a gay person dies, their partner often does not have the right to be the prominent mourner as the family can take over. To correct this, power of attorney can be signed over to one's partner before death. The lack of community and family support can be significant and can have a devastating effect on the bereaved partner. The most successful way to get through the grieving process is to have family and friends bear witness with you and simply 'be there'. To be deprived of this support is cruel and not to have your loss acknowledged by your family is an added burden on top of already unbearable grief.

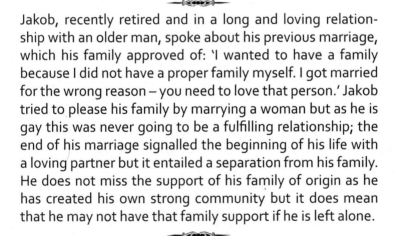

Jakob, recently retired and in a long and loving relation-ship with an older man, spoke about his previous marriage, which his family approved of: 'I wanted to have a family because I did not have a proper family myself. I got married for the wrong reason – you need to love that person.' Jakob tried to please his family by marrying a woman but as he is gay this was never going to be a fulfilling relationship; the end of his marriage signalled the beginning of his life with a loving partner but it entailed a separation from his family. He does not miss the support of his family of origin as he has created his own strong community but it does mean that he may not have that family support if he is left alone.

Loss of identity can also be an issue in later life. A gay retired person in a nursing home may gradually have their identity eroded away as their sexuality is not acknowledged.

———◦◦◦———

Tanya says: 'Just because you are elderly, you do not forget who you are. You have a right to your sexuality right up to the day you die.' Tanya is adamant that a right to sexuality is a human and civil right. The straight community does not want to face the sexuality of people in later life, much less the possibility of gay sexuality. Tanya suggests that it is not up to the gay person to make others aware and it should not be presumed that everyone is straight.

———◦◦◦———

Same-sex couples tend to be much more open about their sexuality – an issue that is often negotiated from the beginning of their relationship. Fidelity is not necessarily assumed and sexual activity is something that can be agreed and then re-negotiated at a number of later points in the relationship. Roles in the relationship can be gender-typed or not as the couple decides and while this can be very freeing it may also mean that the relationship is not as clearly understood by family and friends as those in the straight community. Connection with children or grandchildren may be something that is not available to same-sex couples and this may be a source of sadness or loss. However, like most couples the relationship issues are similar and the struggles familiar.

———◦◦◦———

Jakob says: 'As we are both retired it is possible to spend too much time together. We both have interests of our own and are lucky enough to have a big enough house where we can have independence. I do not let myself think of the potential loss of my partner should he die; if I brood over it, it is bad for me.'

———◦◦◦———

Same-sex couples can regularly face harassment from the public, are not supported in being affectionate in public, are often exiled from religious services and can be disengaged or disowned by their families. That same-sex unions can survive and thrive in spite of these challenges is a testimony to their resilience and to the strength of their relationship.

A Final Word

Because the evolution of the human race has depended on our ability to form relationships and be part of social groups, our genetic heritage is one wherein these skills are finely honed and embedded. For many of us, our lives are busy and we get by in our relationships until, upon retirement, we have to face each other. Often it is only then that we have to search for the knowledge and skills to make those relationships the best they can be. It is never too late to learn something new and never too late to learn more about happiness.

Chapter 5

Sex After 60

Sex after 60 is not the most discussed topic in the world; in fact one might think that there was not much sex after 60 given how little public attention it gets. This is clearly not true but perhaps there is a need to be more open about it so that the large section of the population to whom this applies does not feel so abandoned and invisible. Jane Juska, in her ground-breaking book *A Round-Heeled Woman*,[34] takes on the topic of sex at 66 in a humorous and honest way.

Juska placed an ad in a newspaper which read 'Before I turn 67 – next March – I would like to have a lot of sex with a man I like. If you want to talk first, Trollope works for me.' The book details her experiences and reflections following this advert and it is a graphic, funny and moving account of everything to do with dating, intimacy and rejection. Her bravery is admirable, as is her energy and enthusiasm for pursuing the opposite sex – an effort that might seem over the top to many retired people.

When asked about their sex lives, drives and desires, the people interviewed for this book were for the most part not shy and in fact had quite a lot to say about it. Men, in general, are seekers of more sex, adventure and intimacy.

—◈—

Jake (80 next birthday) said he had been a lover of women all his life and that now, with the aid of Viagra, he planned and appreciated his monthly sexual encounters with women. However, these women tended to be much younger than him.

Tim (a widower of twenty years) said that his quest and lust for women has never abated but that now at 87 he finds relationships easier to manage as 'people know what they want.'

Denis (in his 60s), driven by the desire to be happy and to be special to someone, found the courage to start a new relationship.

—◈—

Women have a more complex response to the question of sex. Those in relationships, for the large part, tend to value the intimacy but sometimes struggle with the changes in their desires and their physical and emotional responses. Single women have not given up on their sexuality but question the effort and risks attached to developing an intimate relationship. Many said that they fear showing their bodies now that they are no longer young, and the fear of rejection is also off-putting. One woman spoke of her mother:

—◈—

'My parents always slept naked together, but when my Dad was in his 70s his desire for sex abated and he was not a man to try drugs such as Viagra. My mother, after four glasses of wine, would mourn loudly, "Where's the passion gone? That's what I want to know! Where's the passion?"'

—❖—

Couples often have to re-broach the thorny topic of sex after retirement as excuses of work stress and lack of time are no longer valid. Many couples avoid the topic and assume that the other person is not interested.

—❖—

Maurice (67) was in a car crash and when he survived had the courage to declare that he no longer wanted to live without sex; he and his wife had not had sex for 35 years. He told his wife that he wanted to leave the relationship only to then be astounded to hear her say in return that she had thought he was the one who was not interested in sex and, as a result, had not said anything for all those years. They have now been happily intimate together for many years.

—❖—

Very often, we assume we know our partner's position on intimacy and out of habit or fear do not question or challenge that assumption. However, assumptions can be dangerous, and so, if you have questions, you should voice them. Be warned, though – if you ask a question, you must be prepared to hear the answer fully, even if it is not what you want to hear.

Many men say they would like more adventurous, kinky or playful sex as they get older but they fear ridicule or rejection from their partner if they propose this. Women often want the security and closeness that sex brings but might be a little intimidated by the suggestions of kinky sex from their partners. On the other hand, many women are relieved to discover that they are still desired and are very open to meeting their partners half way.

Intimacy can be very daunting. Letting another person inside your skin – letting them meet who you really are, as opposed to who you present to the world – is not for the faint-hearted. Taking responsibility for your own desires may also be challenging. Moreover, finding answers to the difficulties that can arise may require knowledge and help. But a person who both takes responsibility and is confident enough to ask for help probably achieves their goal of sexual intimacy. Those who live in their comfort zones may live safely but will not be truly known or appreciated and may miss out on playfulness and pleasure.

Retirement is often a time when people take stock and review their lives and relationships. If there has been no sex in the relationship (or no relationship) then this pause in life offers an opportunity to change tack.

━━◆◇◆━━

Jane and Michael had separated more than once in their relationship, but were brave enough to take on their sexual difficulties when both of them retired. They devoted time and effort (not to mention lots of arguments) to sorting out their intimacy and, a year later, renewed their vows in a playful and joyous manner.

Denis had lived for many years with no sex in his relation-ship, but retirement offered him a chance to let go of his former relationship (with agreement and grace) and take the risk of entering a new relationship. Now he describes himself as a man renewed and alive.

Maura had always experienced sexual difficulties due to unwanted sexual attention as a child. Eventually, as a

retired woman she found the freedom to express herself
sexually and to get the help she knew she needed.

—————

Many retired people speak of gaining a sense of freedom
from society's rules and restrictions and this 'carefree-
ness' extends to the area of sex; not only in the act of
having sex but in how. There is less of a need to have an
orgasm as the aim is intimacy. Also, there is more time
for love-making as it now takes longer for the body to
respond; while there is less urgency there can be more
pleasure and connection. As people come to know and
trust both each other and themselves more, a sense of
peace and acceptance replaces results-driven sex.

However there are also many difficulties that occur
and this next section will look at some of the more
common problems for both individuals and couples.

Men's Sexual Difficulties

Men can experience sexual difficulties at many times
in their lives but there is no doubt that getting older
presents added problems. Often the mind is willing but
the body is weak. Erectile difficulties are not uncom-
mon and can often be a sign of underlying medical
difficulties such as diabetes or heart problems. A man
experiencing sexual difficulties for the first time should
always check with his GP before looking for other solutions. Men are often reluctant to seek help owing to
feelings of embarrassment or fear and thus risk letting
health issues become serious. Seeking help can both
prevent potential problems and address sexual issues
– thus improving the quality of life across the board.

As a man gets older it can take much longer for him
to achieve an erection. This can have a profoundly

negative effect as the man will then begin to worry and think too much about his performance. This focuses his attention on himself and his body may go into defensive mode and refuse to function. He may then begin to anticipate further problems. All of this increases the degree of self-doubt he has and in turn tenses his body, making it less likely to perform on demand. The fear of humiliation can mean that the man avoids intimate encounters and he may turn to pornography (usually on the internet) for comfort. Porn in itself presents many issues, not least because of its addictive nature and the endless possibilities it presents. If a man has been a regular porn user but has hidden this from his partner, he may have developed sexual practices or fantasies that require more stimulation as he gets older. He may find that getting an erection requires specific stimulus that he may be ashamed of and this can alienate him from his current or possible future partners. For example, a man may find cross-dressing erotic and the effort of keeping this from his partner may become an incredible strain as they spend more time together in retirement.

Delayed orgasm and inhibited ejaculation are also common difficulties experienced by older men. In fact, older men can experience what women have known for a long time – that it is not necessary to orgasm during every sexual encounter in order to enjoy the experience. It is common for older men to orgasm perhaps every third or fourth sexual encounter but this lack is often made up for by the slow, sensual and connecting experience that sex can become.

Men's erections also undergo change. A young man can expect his erection to point to the ceiling but an older man's erection may point to the wall or even the floor and still be functional. Older men require more physical stimulation to remain erect and this is not something to worry about. It is unlikely that the penis will be as rigid or hard as it had been in a man's early life. Also, semen is more likely to seep out instead of shooting out as it would have in his earlier experiences.

Often men have a perfectly happy sex life until a change happens. Perhaps he has become separated, divorced or widowed, and the sudden weight of expectation is on him. As he seeks a new partner he may fear rejection or criticism. This is even more difficult if his partner has had an affair as this may erode his confidence, and his faith in his body may take a dive. Luckily, there are medications that can help and Viagra in particular has revolutionised the sexual life of men. However, medication should only be taken in conjunction with a visit to your GP as other medical conditions need to be considered when deciding what medication is best suited to each individual. There are also non-medical solutions to erectile problems, such as pumps and implants, and these can be availed of from a urologist. An important caveat on this topic is to warn against buying medications online. As there is no guarantee as to their content they may cause harm.

Liam (67) began a new relationship with a woman he deeply wanted to impress. To quell his fears he took medication to help him in the sexual arena. The medication worked well initially but he then began to depend on it to the point where he feared trusting his body without it. He did not tell his partner and began to obsess about her finding out and deeming him less of a man. The fear and cover-up began to have a detrimental effect on the relationship and they almost broke up. When he finally told her, his partner was open, compassionate and more than willing to help. Their intimacy improved, and the relationship is now a closer and more honest one.

———❦———

While medication has been of enormous benefit to some men, it has put pressure on others. If a man's partner expects him to use medication but he does not want to have, or has no desire for, sex then he can feel cornered and confused. There is a growing awareness that some men do not desire their partner; that is not to say that they do not love their partners but they may have no sexual response to them. What can make this even more confusing is that the man may have a sexual response to other people or to pornography. This is a very difficult situation to deal with and it may require professional help. There is no doubt that many people, including couples, live happily without sex but with plenty of emotional intimacy. The difficulty is in not being truthful about the situation – where both parties are left guessing and feeling rejected.

For further reading on this topic, Bernie Zilbergeld's *The New Male Sexuality* is a source of information and help for men with sexual problems.[35]

Women's Sexual Difficulties

Women too experience sexual difficulties, particularly following menopause or a hysterectomy. The vaginal area can suffer from dryness and less elasticity, as the vaginal walls are affected by declining oestrogen. Many women speak of a dip in libido at menopause and resultant low sexual desire. However, many other post-menopausal women say that there is a liberation and a letting go that can be exciting and freeing. As Jane Juska says of her search for sex, 'I advertised myself without shame, without remorse, without a shade of embarrassment.'[36] Women say that, although the initial drive for sex decreases, if they do engage in sex then the desire arrives shortly after the encounter begins.

Nuala says: 'I don't wake up anymore with a desire for sex but when we start, I get into it pretty quickly and the orgasm now takes longer to reach but it is more intense and satisfying when I get there.'

Lack of desire or lack of arousal can also be the result of habit – perhaps you have simply gotten out of the habit of seeing yourself as a sexual person and it may take some effort to address this. If this is the case, then many things can be done to assist the situation: reading erotic material such as Nancy Friday's collections of women's fantasies,[37] watching romantic movies, wearing sensual clothes, having a massage or masturbating in comfort all help towards re-awakening the sensual self. However, many older women speak of physical pain and discomfort when having intercourse and this can be a serious deterrent to intimacy. Lubricants and localised hormones can help but these should be taken under the guidance of a GP or women's clinic.

As women get older, their bodies become less supple, their midriffs expand and self-criticism can become a barrier to intimacy. Weight too can become a focus of attention and, instead of bringing fun and pleasure, sex can become an exercise in self-recrimination and self-hatred. Clearly this is not an experience that anyone would want to repeat and so self-commentary and self-criticism need to be shed if sex is to be enjoyed fully. Attention in intimacy should always be fully on your partner. Very simply, this means giving full attention to your partner by focusing your senses, using touch, taste, smell, sound and sight. If your attention is on your partner then there will not be any focus on criticising your own body, and this has to be freeing. A body that is subject to an endless diatribe of not being good enough will hardly be in a position to express itself fully and appreciate pleasure.

Karen says: 'More effort needs to go into sex: dim lights, music, etc. You have to go back to a situation where you were very happy with foreplay and nothing else. Desire comes back more so in specific situations like weekends away or holidays.'

Illness and restricted mobility interfere with intercourse but if any effort is put in it is rewarded handsomely. The saying 'use it or lose it' has relevance here as we often take the easy way out. It is much easier to put off sex rather than plan and implement a sensuous session that might require physical, emotional and mental preparation. Sex reminds us that we are alive. It can take us out of our comfort zones and express the playful and fearless side of ourselves. Embarrassment may have to be overcome and physical realities accepted, e.g. urinary incontinence is often a fact of life and planning for this (by using a dark towel or pad) may be necessary. The wonderful thing about a sex life in retirement is that it helps us to cast off the burdens of fear, criticism and shame, while allowing us to practise fun, determination and self-care.

There are many books on women's sexual health.
One to try is *Sex Matters for Women.*[38]

Starting a New Sexual Relationship

Forty-five per cent of women aged 65 or older are
widows[39] and in the Western world we have growing
numbers of people living alone – divorced, widowed
and long-term single people all face the possibility of
going back to dating in later life. This prospect can be
both intimidating and scary. Some choose not to get
into a sexual relationship as they find enough fulfilment in their relationships with family and friends. For
others, the desire for partnership is still very strong
and they are not ready to give up on sex. When an
older woman decides to pursue a sexual relationship,
she has to consider the effect it will have on others:
adult children, grandchildren, relations and friends.
She may have to face disapproval and disparagement
and the support she needs may be lacking. Possible
partners too may be difficult to find as traditionally
men seek women who are younger than them. Thus,
an older woman seeking a new sexual mate will need
to have courage, confidence and faith. The etiquette of
internet dating may have to be learned and the risks
of rejection managed and survived, but for those brave
enough, the reward is often worth it.

Lena (67) began a relationship with a man twenty years
older than her and while her family and friends all warned
against it, they have been happy together for ten years.
She moved in with him when he was 82 and they are both
healthy and happy now five years on.

Men too face the enormous difficulty of taking the plunge into a new sexual relationship following divorce or death of a spouse. The old fears of rejection and judgement again come to the surface and it requires courage and action to overcome these fears. The first step is always the most vital: engage with others and go to places where there may be attractive potential partners. The easy route will always be to stay at home with the TV for company but you will be rewarded if you push yourself to step into the world of relationships. Ask someone for coffee as this is less daunting than dinner or a drink and it does not assume any potentially embarrassing questions such as 'Do I kiss or not?' Take it slowly but be determined that you will meet someone for whom you will overcome your fear of embarrassment. Remember honesty is a very attractive quality so letting your potential partner know of your fears will only make you more endearing to them.

Habits and Patterns

Couples can experience problems with their sex lives on retirement as it often brings to light habits and patterns that have existed for years beforehand. Sometimes, the availability of impotency drugs forces the couple to address a habit of non-sexuality and one or both of them might be reluctant to do this. Many people assume that their partner is happy with the sex life, or non-sex life, they share and this unchallenged assumption can lead to a distancing, or even resentment, in the relationship.

Following retirement, June said that what she would miss most was the male companionship and closeness of her colleagues and clients as her husband had no desire for sex and had built a very separate life from her. Her sense of hurt and anger at this had no outlet for expression and she feared where this might lead.

———❖———

Sometimes there is a large imbalance in levels of libido and desire and one partner can feel frustrated while the other is deliberately oblivious. If this is not tackled then the couple can replace intimacy with bickering and snide remarks. Fighting and arguing is a form of intimacy as the couple focus the full force of attention on each other; however it can lead to a very destructive relationship with the intensity concentrated on negativity. It is never too late to change our patterns and it only takes one person to be aware of, and courageous enough to challenge, the pattern. When people opt for a 'quiet life' in a bid to avoid any possible disagreements, this can mean that neither partner is heard or understood. As a result, both partners may begin to look outside the relationship for connection – perhaps to golf, book clubs, the pub or other outlets.

What is important here is that you take responsibility for your own happiness. If you are aware that there is a lack of physical or emotional intimacy then it is your job to initiate change and challenge the pattern. Changing the location of the conversation can assist. For example, discussing sex while out to dinner or out for a walk on the beach can elicit a different response, making possible a more open discussion. Asking questions rather than blaming or demanding can be very helpful in getting your partner to partake in the conversation. Being open to trying out creative solutions will break the rigid pattern that may have developed.

Finally, there is an assumption that older people are not sexual and this myth finds its way into social policies, advertising and the media. Homes for the elderly have few double rooms and, for the large part, most individuals have single beds, making a sexual encounter even more difficult as falling out of bed can have serious consequences for brittle bones. As our over-65 population is set to increase by 33 per cent in the next ten years,[40] this ageism needs to be addressed. Facilities, information, support and advertising will all need to focus on this large part of the population so that they can avail of a rich and full life. If older people speak openly and confidently about their sex lives and desires then perhaps there will be a corresponding shift in policies and consciousness. It means being bold and brave but it is undoubtedly worth pursuing.

Chapter 6

Spirituality

Spirituality and religion have enormously different meanings for different people but the search for meaning can be an important focus of development in the retired stage of life. As death approaches and attendance at funerals becomes part of the social routine, the inevitability of the end of this life has to be faced. The part that religion and religious practices play in a person's life varies from person to person, but those who adhere to their practices appear to gain much in terms of happiness and connection. While religious practices can be public, spirituality is often very private and personal and yet can be the mainstay of a person's life. It gives meaning to everyday existence and can be intuited in a person's every action and response. This chapter does not advocate any particular religious viewpoint but does refer to some of the literature on the effect of spiritual practices on people's well-being. Perhaps the most potent source of information on the topic comes from the interviewees themselves. The myriad of spiritual positions they adopt and the advice they proffer for the soon-to-be-retired are worthy of consideration.

Search for Meaning

To begin, let us consider the differences between spirituality and religion. Religion is the organised practice of a particular creed whereas spirituality is described as one's personal relationship with the meaning of life. Religion offers guidelines and practices – usually refined over centuries according to record or scripture – that offer a way of living directed towards a particular goal, e.g. everlasting life.

Spiritual practice may evolve from our struggle to understand what life is about or, to put it another way, it becomes a search for meaning. This may involve soul-searching and engaging with existential questions: What does it mean to be alive? Why is there something rather than nothing? How can I live a worthwhile life? What will happen after I die? What do I know and accept?

While particular religions have ready answers to the above questions, you may find that you come to experience these answers through spiritual practice. To experience knowledge, as opposed to having an intellectual understanding, requires practices such as stillness, meditation and prayer. Understanding ourselves and our relationship with human existence can become interesting topics for further reflection as we reach retirement age and have more time to ponder such themes.

Most people, by the time they have hit their 50s, have experienced the loss of someone close to them or the loss of something that is important to them. This confronts people with the question of how to cope with loss and how to make sense of grief in the face of the increasing losses of later life. Some of these inevitable losses include loss of parents, spouse/partner or a very close family member; loss of job, career, reputation or occupation; loss of physical wellness, attractiveness or agility; loss of children to emigration or distance; loss of friends to death or Alzheimer's disease; and loss of mental ability, memory or interest. Grief is part and parcel of life and retirement is the time when it appears to be ever-present.

In order to face such painful challenges, we need to foster a strong and resilient sense of what life is about. If our religion offers us a life after this one then we can take solace in the knowledge that our suffering has a purpose and an end. Such religious belief is not for everyone. Sometimes religious practice can seem routine, habitual and unconnected to us in our vulnerability and need. If this is so, it may be important to look to spiritual practices to see how they can help us withstand struggles and defeat futility and hopelessness.

As a character in Jeffery Eugenides' book *The Marriage Plot* says, the effect of analysing the religious experience of famous men and women made him 'aware of the centrality of religion in human history and, more important, of the fact that religious feeling didn't arise from going to church or reading the Bible but from the most private interior experiences, either of great joy or of staggering pain'.[41]

Liz (late 50s) describes her journey and what helped her:

'I had always loved the church and found solace in sitting in the quietness and peace of the late evening with the smell of incense in the air. However, when I reached my mid-teens, I felt that my religion was too distant and it made me feel guilty about my desires and my body. I discovered meditation and Advaita [the ancient Indian Vedic tradition] and it opened up a new sense of connection and self-compassion for me. In a strange way it allowed me to connect more honestly with my religion of birth.'

Liz began her practice of meditation in the early 1990s and, while initially finding it difficult to sit quietly for half an hour twice a day, she soon discovered the enormous benefits of stillness.

Stillness is central to most religions and many spiritual practices. When the mind quiets down, true knowledge can surface in its own time. Again, to quote the character from Eugenides' book:

'He realised that the mystics were all saying the same thing. Enlightenment came from the extinction of desire. Desire didn't bring fulfilment but only temporary satiety until the next temptation came along. And that was only if you were lucky enough to get what you wanted. If you didn't, you spent your life in unrequited longing.'[42]

Liz found that with the practice of meditation deepening, she was able to observe herself better and not just react to all that life was throwing at her. With practice, she began to see how she always resorted to the same habits to deal with her insecurities and how this always led to familiar paths of unhappiness:

'I would feel horrible about my weight and the desire to look better would drive me to self-loathing and deprivation. When that did not work, I would binge eat and go shopping – a merry-go-round of shame and guilt. Now I am amused when I see the desires coming up – I know that I need to meditate and this will stop the self-commentary and the desire.'

——⟨◆◇◆⟩——

A major benefit for Liz was a reconnection to her own Christian religion. She found that she had a deeper understanding of one of her favourite lines from scripture, 'Be still and know that I am God.'[43] Through achieving stillness, she says that she has begun to feel a deep connection to the divine within and that the sense of separateness is lessening with each passing year.

Self-Discipline and Self-Discovery

Spiritual practices range from yoga, meditation and mindfulness to prayer, connection with nature and ritual. All require self-discipline and practice as, without continued practice, no real change can occur. We often perceive self-discipline as punishment leading to cycles of determination followed by failure. But in a religious sense self-discipline is to be a disciple – a follower – of something. To be a follower of self-discovery, of finding a true sense of who we are, is surely worth the effort. To commit to a spiritual practice is to commit to one's self. Holding this in mind is a form of self-care, making it easier to be disciplined and optimistic. Such practice can fortify and protect us against life's difficulties while opening up a truer sense of who we are.

Marianne Williamson's well-quoted words highlight the importance of this:

'Our deepest fear is not that we are inadequate. Our deepest fear is that we are powerful beyond measure. ... As we let our own light shine, we unconsciously give other people permission to do the same. As we are liberated from our fear, our presence automatically liberates others.'[44]

Overcoming fear, discovering who we really are and finding a purpose and meaning in life are some of our most important human endeavours. It is often our experience that we are too busy making a living and caring for the next generation to give much attention to this in our earlier lives but later life creates an opportunity for reflective exploration. If we do not nurture and develop a practice of becoming still, it can be challenging to break out of the habitual ways of thinking and being, embedded in our daily routine. It is generally accepted that we need 'good company' to support us in this journey towards self-discovery. Spending time with others in search of spirituality is not only supportive, it increases and deepens the effect of the experience. Retreats, workshops and weekly practice meetings can help maintain a practice, raise questions and offer the benefit of others' struggles and experiences.

Liz says: 'For twenty years I meditated with a group once a week. Not only was this always the best meditation of the week but the group became soulmates, challengers and fellow seekers. I trust them completely.'

Coping Ability and Spirituality

For many, the ability to cope with life's difficulties is closely linked to their spirituality or religion. As Boyd Lemon says in his book, *Retirement: A Memoir and Guide*:

'I choose to believe, to the contrary, that there is a supreme force that controls the universe, and that I am part of it and in some way will be for eternity. Why do I believe this? Because it feels true to me. Call it belief, or faith or maybe wishful thinking.'[45]

However, what people mean by spirituality can vary hugely, from close connection to a particular religion to a deep connection to nature, or to a personal practice of meditation. A report in *Scientific American* by Sandra Upson[46] states that having a strong connection to a religion seriously boosts your capacity to cope in difficult situations:

'A large body of research suggests that, as compared with religious individuals, people who lack a creed are less likely to be healthy and happy – surely the two most important earthly concerns – and tend to lose out on at least seven years of life, some estimates suggest.'[47]

One of the major benefits of belonging to a religious group is attachment to a community of like-minded individuals who invite you into their social circle and offer a sense of belonging. Research suggests, however, that those people who are loosely connected to their religion are 'actually less happy than avowed atheists'.[48] Anne Davis, in her thesis on the psychological effects of religion and spirituality, expresses the view that particular types of religious activity, such as attendance at church services, consistently relate to greater subjective life satisfaction and well-being. However, if there is a struggle with one's religion it can actually have a negative effect:

'Furthermore, negative religious coping styles such as difficulty forgiving God have been related to negative mental health outcomes such as increased depression, stress and suicidal behaviour.'[49]

It is important in the light of this to have a robust and engaged relationship with religion. Our beliefs and practices need to be open to challenge and questioning so that we have something truly potent in our lives; suggestions for spiritual expansion are listed at the end of this chapter.

Adversity and Spiritual Resilience

While it is true that a strong connection to religion offers contentment and certainty, there is growing evidence that this mostly works if the society in which the person lives supports this connection. In the Western world there has been a fall-off in attendance at church services – at least partially related to scandals in the Catholic Church – and the societal support for religion may have lessened as a result. A move towards a more personal spirituality has grown over the past decade with a huge growth in Eastern spirituality and an emphasis on having a personalised connection with God. Davis notes that, for some, this transition has been extremely difficult and has resulted in a conflictual relationship with the religion of their birth. As she has discovered:

'Conflictual religiosity was a unique predictor of panic disorder even when accounting for state anxiety, hypochondriacal beliefs, abnormal illness behaviour and irrational thinking. In particular, people who experienced more religious guilt and felt unable to meet religious expectations or cope with religious fears were more likely to suffer from panic disorders.'[50]

This implies that being focused on and content with one's religious and/or spiritual practice can protect against experiencing heightened anxiety or fear. The research concludes that having a strong sense of spirituality offers us good coping skills for life, particularly in the face of adversity. Women, in general, seem to be more likely than men to talk about their religious coping strategies and are more likely to participate in church or spiritual activities. Spiritual or religious connections can offer many volunteering opportunities and this participation can support feelings of usefulness and offer a meaningful contribution to society – a purpose worth nurturing.

Sadie, a retired woman from the missionaries, says that the sense of community in the Church is very important to her: 'I have time to go to talks on mystics. There are lovely liturgies in Ireland with links from readings to life. I'm new in Dublin and looking for people to connect with and this I do through my faith experience – it gives me a good anchor. There is a sense that you can talk to the person beside you but I wish there was more tea and coffee here.'

Research indicates that people who express their spirituality through their religious beliefs have both greater spiritual health and a greater immunity to stressful situations than those who indicated that they were spiritual with no set of religious beliefs.[51] This effect of relatively high subjective well-being held true for all religions, such as Buddhism, Christianity, Hinduism and Islam – but in non-religious societies (Nordic countries in particular) people's spirits were just as high. Sandra Upson concludes that:

'Religion can certainly help people to be happier, but other things can help you do the same thing. A peaceful cooperative society, even in the absence of religion, seems to have the same effect.'[52]

Observations of older adults have shown increased reflection, less concern for material things and more interest in satisfaction with life. By later life, many older adults may have experiences that seem mystical – these may be responses to illness or other challenges – and may experience an expanded sense of time. This enables retired people to devote more time and energy to spiritual activities such as meditation, prayer, connection to nature, poetry or reflection. To quote John Ruskin:

'To watch the corn grow, and the blossoms set; to draw hard breath over ploughshare or spade; to read, to think, to love, to hope, to pray – these are the things that make men happy.'[53]

Making Sense of Life and Death

As we become more aware of mortality, the task is to find a way to make sense of how the body declines and how we cope with these changes in an accepting way. We need to adjust our lives to accommodate these changes and allow ourselves to 'slow down'. We also have to cope with friends and family members dying and manage the loss of things we used to take for granted.

Retirement can catapult such issues to the forefront of our minds and create challenges to our daily existence as we move towards the later life stage.

Clare (a counsellor in her late 50s) reports that her crux came when she had children and the question of what religious culture to rear them in became an issue. She says: 'What did we really believe in, rearing children? What were our values regarding life and the universe and how would we impart that outside organised religion? We chose the Church of Ireland as the culture we lived in was predominately Christian.' Clare says that she was always drawn to the Eastern, Buddhist way of doing things and that this is what has sustained her in life. Like many people she felt the absence of a ready community and found that she 'had to create my own community' of like-minded people. This has worked well in sustaining her through life.

A more personalised approach to a relationship with God also sustains many people. Admitting doubts and questions, Maureen (84) reflects:

'I can't make up my mind. I have a sneaking feeling that nothing happens [after death] but I wouldn't feel right if I didn't ask for help to get through the day – it works, I feel I get the help.'

Many people speak of spirituality deepening after retirement – that is to say that whatever approach a person has before retirement is likely to continue with more emphasis after retirement. Ned (84 and retired from business) says that his faith made a big difference on retirement:

'It relieved me of all the tensions and problems at retirement, including tax inspectors chasing me. I firmly believe in God and a supreme being – how else could the world have come about?'

However, for others, this comfort is not as readily available. Tim, whose wife died suddenly twenty years ago, found no solace in religion. He says that his experience of the Church as a young man was critical and negative and he looks instead to love and relationships for meaning in life. At the age of twenty, he went to confession and told the priest he had had sex. The response was, 'people like you shouldn't be in this country.' Tim said he obliged by joining the merchant navy and travelling the world. He feels that questioning is the most important thing in life and suggests, 'Maybe it sounds a bit selfish, but do what you want to do without hurting any people.' This is the approach that has sustained him.

At 88, Tim has witnessed a lot of loss and says that he doesn't think about dying: 'Most of my family are gone so I don't have to worry about their sadness when I die. I will give my body to science and then, when it is cremated, my ashes can be scattered in the Dodder River and in the sea. We come from the sea and I'm happy to be returned to it.' Tim shows a great sense of acceptance and peace in his philosophy of life and indeed death.

Taboos on Talking About Spirituality and Death

Many of the interviewees had thought deeply about dying and the next life but most said that they struggled to speak of this to their friends or children. Dave, whose life partner has been ill for a long time, speaks freely with her about life and death but there is a sense that children need to develop their own relationship with their understanding of their spirituality:

'There is a conversation every few weeks – how did the hospital visit go? There is an increasing involvement and awareness and a responsiveness regarding things that need to be done.'

This is both practical and reassuring for both of them, even if it is challenging.

Ian, a retired businessman, experienced a new understanding of how to speak about morality and spirituality with his adult children following a trip to America. He said that he was impressed by how open families were about their dedication to very clear values: 'Their reason for doing things is known, repeated and understood.' He remembers facing his own blocks when attending a parenting course many years ago when the issue of suicide in young men came up for discussion: 'Fear and protection of kids led to not speaking.' However, he and his wife discussed mortality and found a way of raising the issue lightly with their son. He finds that he is constantly questioning and that this tendency has increased since the children left home: 'These kind of questions are hugely difficult – I seem to reject the

Church in part yet wonder if you can do what you like and
have no impact.'

—◦◦◦—

Some parents may not want to impose their religion or
faith on their children, but almost all want to offer at
least strong moral guidelines. Parents may not want to
confer their uncertainties and fears on their offspring
but this can lead to silence and a lack of discussion of,
and exploration around, religious or spiritual themes.
Both parents and adult children should consider risking
a conversation about spirituality or religion with each
other with faith that both parties will be strong enough
for such an encounter. Death, religion and spirituality
are not something to fear and sweep under the carpet
but are worthy of discussion and respectful expression. Practising courage and faith in the potential of
others is in itself a spiritual practice and is perhaps the
epitome of respect.

Coping With Death and Loss

Coping with death and the loss of loved ones has been
alluded to earlier in this chapter. Being able to talk
about death and loss seems to offer consolation and
the rituals around death and loss can offer consolation
and structure.

—◦◦◦—

Aisling (retired ten years) says: 'As you get older you see all
of the people you know die – how do you not think about
it?' She has held the hands of friends as they died and told
them they were free to go; she found much comfort in this.
She and her friends now talk about 'which one of us will go
next' and she says that everyone has thought about this.

Tom (recently retired) says that he would 'love to believe in re-embodiment' but that, 'the more I try to hang on to a belief the less I believe it.' He says that spirituality was the thing that kept him going for many years but that now he is questioning if he needs it as much. He recommends not getting stuck on one path but looking into different traditions and being open to what is on offer.

Dave encourages reflection although he says that it 'can be threatening to explore – a shaking of the foundations.' He says: 'For me it is an opportunity. I always kept spirituality going – moving from a very institutionalised area to a much more personal, explorative type of approach. What kicked this off was poetry – it really rocked my boat. Poets develop and articulate our doubts and explorations. I see spirituality as an extension of myself. I would not accept authority (or organised church) anyway.'

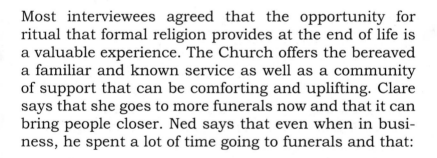

Most interviewees agreed that the opportunity for ritual that formal religion provides at the end of life is a valuable experience. The Church offers the bereaved a familiar and known service as well as a community of support that can be comforting and uplifting. Clare says that she goes to more funerals now and that it can bring people closer. Ned says that even when in business, he spent a lot of time going to funerals and that:

'They provide solace and a space in which to meet and connect with people. I know that religion is important to a lot of my friends but we do not talk about it specifically. We would not want to offend someone with strong anti-religious feelings.'

Aisling expresses the view that the rural Church still offers a huge sense of community support and that this is very healthy. She also adds, however, that it does not necessarily follow that everyone will be connected – you can be very isolated if you hold a different view to the community. She states:

———❧———

'I do not want a priest pontificating at my funeral. It is natural to want to be at peace with ourselves – it means finding some equilibrium and it does not matter where that comes from. Call it spirituality or acceptance; it is finding pleasure in every day. Yes, there is a God but that God is all around us.'

———❧———

She says that she would like to be cremated and has spoken to friends about this. Talking seems to present a huge difficulty when it comes to acknowledging death with family and friends. As Bridget Megarry advises:

'Let's try to be a bit more honest and start talking about this thing called death and learn to treat it as a reality so that we can prepare ourselves through shared experiences and common wisdom. I have travelled all my life but this is the hardest and loneliest journey I have ever made.'[54]

The loss of friends and family through death, coupled with the loneliness of illness or infirmity, can test even the most spiritual of people. Angela Neustatter helps us consider how to cope with such challenges:

'I realise that the simplicity of the lifestyle that I have equals contentment. A far happier state than

I could have contemplated, this fading down, and it surprises me to be able to say that I may be on the cusp of 70 but perhaps this too can be a decade of gain, so that at the end I will say – as the poet May Sarton did on her 80th birthday – "I am more myself than ever."[55]

Practices to Instil Spirituality

Many people have a highly developed sense of spirituality and are living examples of 'lightness of being'. But there is no doubt that, for many, retirement might be the first time that there has been time to consider which spiritual path to follow. Below are some suggestions on how to begin that journey.

Seeking

Be a seeker of who you really are, ask questions and look for answers from the wisdom that is readily available (scriptures, writings, poetry, etc.). Put the wisdom into practice and let your own experience tell you the truth.

Stillness

Learning how to still the mind is at the core of most spiritual practice and most people need direction in learning how to do this. Go to meditation/mindfulness/yoga/prayer group classes and learn from experienced people first. Then, practise until it becomes natural to you – this can take years.

Self-Discipline

Be a follower of your practice and realise that most things worth having are difficult. Be compassionate with yourself and start gently and in pace with where you are at.

Good Company

The support of other seekers is not to be ignored. Being in the company of people who stretch us and who are on the same journey is invaluable. Go to retreats, join a weekly group, have discussions, challenge and rant.

Lighten Up

Spiritual people tend to be light-hearted and good to be around. They are not judgemental or righteous. They know that much of what worries us is an illusion and are therefore not bothered by it. Just by remembering to 'lighten up' moves us further along the road of enlightenment.

Finally, some of the words of wisdom from the interviewees on this topic:

'Ask what you want out of your life. Do not put things off as you may not live to enjoy it.'

'Live the best you can; be happy. Don't wish evil on people of any kind.'

'Question and enjoy the reflection.'

'Start at pre-retirement stage – calm down, step back from the madness. Get up on the balcony and think about what's going on.'

'Insist that colleagues go to retirement courses – get them talking.'

'Have an open mind. Talk to people about spirituality.'

'It does matter to us – spirituality is part of coping and part of who we are.'

'Take an interest in faith, practise it and it will give purpose to life.'

'Accept the loss of your standing in the community and look to your achievements and not your disappointments.'

'Feel privileged. Take the opportunity for genuine spiritual-ity and healing – know that God can work even in difficult times.'

'Why regret things not done when the future still offers so much to do?'

The people interviewed for this book have found ways of making sense of both life and death and, in the process, find their spirituality alive and well. This experience is evidenced in everything from nature and literature to mindfulness and organised religion. All come across as people in the process of living and making sense of life; all are hungry for meaning and many have achieved a state of contentment – in spite of the losses along the way. We all need to move along this journey.

Chapter 7

Acceptance, Fun and Irreverence

If you are retired and lucky enough to find yourself financially secure, mentally and physically fit, and in a good relationship, then it is time to indulge in fun, pass on your wisdom and fulfil your dreams. There is a sense that those who have lived life have much to offer in terms of wisdom and experience and this should be offered freely and without any need for reward. As it is wisely said in *The Prophet*:

> 'It is well to give when asked, but it is better to give unasked, through understanding;
> And to the open-handed the search for one who shall receive is joy greater than giving.
> And is there aught you would withhold?
> All you have shall some day be given;
> Therefore give now, that the season of giving may be yours and not your inheritors.'[56]

If you are not in the above position of well-being, there is still much you can do: live in the moment, be truly good to yourself (even if this requires discipline) and have faith in your abilities. Learning to detach from all that we have amassed – jobs, relationships, children, possessions and expectations – is far more liberating than you might expect. Detachment is not the same as not caring; it means to be free of desire. Freedom to let things be, to accept with serenity are some of the possibilities of later life. To quote Leonard Cohen speaking at one of his concerts in Dublin in 2011:

'I have studied all the theologies and all the philosophies, but cheerfulness keeps breaking through.'

The Internet As a Way Forward

For those who are lonely and isolated, the internet can offer a beacon of hope. Research in the United States, based on surveys of 8,000 men and women aged 50 and upwards, shows that depression is almost one-third less likely among those who use social networking than among non-users. Indeed, according to the research, the internet helps older people to lead independent lives and to make better informed decisions about travel, health and so on.[57]

The older people get, the greater the risk of loneliness and isolation, and the internet can offer an easy way to stay in contact with people who are abroad and to make new connections. A fear of technology, a resistance to change and the lack of a teacher are some of the factors that can stop this method of connection from happening.

Sophie (83) says of her cousin in the US (aged 78): 'Jim knows more about local gossip than I do. He gets it all from the net. He does all his Christmas shopping online and keeps up to date with what the younger relations would like. He'd like to email me but I've never learned and I feel it is too late now.'

———⟨•⟩———

This book started out with the claim that retirement is a stage of development and that we cannot stop from learning even if we tried – just look at how everyone has adjusted to remote controls, microwaves and mobile phones. We need to extend this confidence to the internet and harness its possibilities for those people in later life. If the internet is conquered, the world can open up; deals can be picked up for weekends away, museums can be visited virtually and chat rooms joined – even in the middle of the night. It is all about not getting stuck in a thought pattern – a thought pattern that repeats 'I can't!' If life has been successfully lived, then many obstacles will have been overcome along the way. So, view this as just one more such obstacle and approach it with determination and faith.

The internet and social media also offer possibilities for exercising the so-called 'grey power'. As the number of retired people increases so does their capacity to address and influence the political, social and media agendas. In Ireland we had a fantastic example of the political power of the retired population when, in 2008, a march on the Dáil was successfully held by a huge number of people protesting the changes to eligibility for the over-70s to the medical card. This demonstrated the political possibilities but the reality is that, for many people in this age group, meeting up to socially agitate is not possible due to physical challenges. The internet offers an alternative route to interact and be heard, but first it has to be mastered. Computer courses are offered in every locality in the country. In many schools transition year students offer one-to-one teaching and it would not cost much to get someone to come to your house to offer a few lessons – any local agency such as an active retirement group or school principal could recommend someone reliable and honest. Being able to connect with others and discuss issues of concern from your own couch or table opens up possibilities for being heard at all levels.

Irreverence

Exercising this 'grey' power may challenge the prevailing idea that older people are problematic and uninterest-ing. It is time to be heard and perhaps an irreverent approach is what is needed. Sometimes, older people are treated as delicate by the media, giving the impres-sion that they need to be handled with kid gloves, but older people come in the same variety as all people: kind, funny, eccentric, belligerent, etc. If they were treated a little more irreverently then perhaps their full scope would be appreciated and good healthy argu-ments had.

Ned (84) enthuses: 'What I love about going to the pub is the possibility of having a good argument. It's even better if it goes on for days or weeks. I don't want people to treat me with kid gloves or "respect". I want people to have a good go at me and I can hold my own.'

Irreverence towards loss of youth, beauty and vitality may also be a useful approach to take as it is inevitable that these things will gradually fade. Lightening up in the face of the inevitable has a freeing perspective and a carefree approach is one of the possibilities that older age offers. This might sound far-fetched to those who are sandwiched between minding very elderly parents and financially strapped adult children but think of how wonderful it would be to approach all of life with a light attitude. It is all achievable if the practices laid out in this book are followed and no doubt we all know examples of such people in our lives – if they can be like that so can we. A poem by Jenny Joseph is the perfect illustration:

Warning
When I am an old woman I shall wear purple
With a red hat which doesn't go, and doesn't suit
   me.
And I shall spend my pension on brandy and
   summer gloves
And satin sandals, and say we've no money for
   butter.
I shall sit down on the pavement when I'm tired
And gobble up samples in shops and press alarm
   bells
And run my stick along the public railings
And make up for the sobriety of my youth.
I shall go out in my slippers in the rain
And pick flowers in other people's gardens
And learn to spit.
You can wear terrible shirts and grow more fat
And eat three pounds of sausages at a go
Or only bread and pickle for a week
And hoard pens and pencils and beermats and
   things in boxes.
But now we must have clothes that keep us dry
And pay our rent and not swear in the street

And set a good example for the children.
We must have friends to dinner and read the
  papers.
But maybe I ought to practice a little now?
So people who know me are not too shocked and
  surprised
When suddenly I am old, and start to wear purple.
– Jenny Joseph[58]

Acceptance

The challenges of later life are many: financial burdens, ill health, loss of independence and death of loved ones. What is needed to meet these challenges is courage, faith, self-esteem, reliance on others and, above all, acceptance. With acceptance comes the capacity to face whatever life is throwing at us and decide how best to respond. Choosing to be dependent on others, to accept the lack of independence and to do this with good humour and lightness are surely divine qualities that are not beyond our reach. A hospice nurse revealed[59] that what many people wish for on their deathbeds is that they had spent more time with friends, and perhaps this is worth listening to. Giving time and attention to people we love, admire and have fun with is not something we can take for granted in later life – we need to invest energy in this through whatever means are available: phone, email, text messaging and meeting up. We sow what we reap, and we must reap well in order to enjoy retirement. As Dave wisely says:

—❧❦❧—

'My wife has been gravely ill for some time and talking and facing it is what we do. You have to go mad and accept it.'

—❧❦❧—

We chose to be who we are and this choice continues right up to the time we exit this life. Choose life, choose fun, choose love, choose fearlessness and choose acceptance.

Endnotes

Preface

[1] TILDA (2011), *Fifty Plus in Ireland 2011: First Results from the Irish Longitudinal Study on Ageing*, Dublin: Trinity College Dublin.

Chapter 1

[2] Murray, M. (2009), 'Realising the True Value of Your Life', *Irish Times*, 21 April, p. 11.

[3] Erikson, E.H. (1959), *Identity and the Life Cycle*, New York: International Universitites Press.

[4] Handy, C. (2012), 'Relationships Ireland – Keynote Speech', Relationships Ireland 50th Anniversary Conference, June, Dublin.

Chapter 2

[5] TILDA (2011).

[6] *Hamlet*, Act II, Scene 2.

[7] TILDA (2011).

[8] TILDA (2011).

[9] TILDA (2011, p. 159).

[10] Alton, B. (2011), *Retirement: An Opportunity to Upgrade Your Health*, Retirement Planning Course, Dublin: Civil Service Training and Development Centre, 113–114.

[11] Gaffney, M. (2007), 'The Pursuit of Happiness', *Irish Times*, 25 August, pp. 18–19.

[12] Magee, A. (2008), 'A Happy Balance', *Red Magazine*, July, pp. 229–232.

13 Donna and Philip Berber, quoted in K. Holmquist (2007) 'Digging Deep', *Irish Times*, Weekend Section, 25 August.
14 Brickman, D., Coates, D. and Janoff-Bulman, R. (1978), 'Lottery Winners and Accident Victims: Is Happiness Relative?', *Journal of Personality and Social Psychology*, 36(8), pp. 917–927.
15 Buettner, D. (2004), *Blue Zone: Lessons for Living Longer from the People Who've Lived the Longest*, New York: National Geographic.
16 Alton (2011).
17 TILDA (2011).

Chapter 3

18 Newman, M. (2007), *Emotional Capitalists: The New Leaders*, Chichester: John Wiley & Sons Ltd.
19 Quoted in Greer, C. (2013), 'What Are You Thinking? (Part Deux)', *Charlie Greer's HVAC Profit Booster*, available from: <http://www.hvacprofitboosters.com/Tips/Tip_Archive/tip_archive7.html> (accessed 28 January 2014).
20 Wehrenberg, M. and Coppersmith, L. (2008), 'Technotrap: When Work Becomes Your Second Home', *Psychotherapy Networker*, pp. 40–45 and 64.
21 Power, C.D. (2012), 'Field of Dreams', Speech delivered at graduation ceremony, John Scottus School, 24 May, Dublin.
22 Covey, S.R. (nd), 'The 90/10 Principle', *Office of Medical Student Affairs, Indiana University*, available from: <http://msa.medicine.iu.edu/files/2713/3236/9537/90-10Principle.pdf> (accessed 8 September 2013).
23 Centre for Clinical Interventions (nd), 'Mindfulness and Letting Go', Centre for Clinical Interventions, available from: <http://www.cci.health.wa.gov.au/docs/ACF3C6F.pdf> (accessed 31 August 2013).

Chapter 4

24 Curtin, J.S. (2002), 'Living Longer, Divorcing Later: The Japanese Silver Divorce Phenomenon', *Global Communications Platform: The Japanese Institute of Global Communications*, available from: <http://www.glocom.org/debates/20020805_curtin_living/> (accessed 20 September 2013).

25 Scheibehenne, B.M., Matta, J. and Todd, P.M. (2011), 'Older But Not Wiser: Predicting a Partner's Preferences Gets Worse With Age', *Journal of Consumer Psychology*, 21(2), pp. 184–191.

26 Gottman, J. (1994), *What Predicts Divorce? The Relationship Between Marital Processes and Marital Incomes*, Hillsdale, NJ: Lawrence Erlbaum Associates; Gottman, J. (1998), 'Psychology and the Study of Marital Processes', *Annual Review of Psychology*, 49, pp. 169–197.

27 Marshall, A. (2010), *How Can I Ever Trust You Again? Infidelity: From Discovery to Recovery in Seven Steps*, London: Bloomsbury Publishing. See also Clark-Flory, T. (2011), 'How Common Is Infidelity, Anyway?', *Salon*, 12 June, available from: <http://www.salon.com/2011/06/12/infidelity_3/> (accessed 3 March 2013).

28 Murray, J.G., Murray, J.D., Swanson, C.C., Tyson, R. and Swanson, K.R. (2002), *The Mathematics of Marriage: Dynamic Nonlinear Models*, Cambridge, MA: MIT Press.

29 Gaffney, M. (2011), *Flourishing*, Dublin: Penguin Ireland.

30 Gallacher, D. and Gallacher, J. (2011), 'Are Relationships Good for Your Health?', *Student British Journal of Medicine*, available from: <http://student.bmj.com/student/view-article.html?id=sbmj.d404> (accessed 28 January 2014).

31 Acevedo, B. and Aron, A. (2009), 'Does a Long-Term Relationship Kill Romantic Love?', *Review of General Psychology*, 13(1), pp. 59–68.

32 Sigle-Rushton, W. (2010), 'Men's Unpaid Work and Divorce: Reassessing Specialization and Trade in British Families', *Feminist Economics*, 16(2), pp. 1–26.

33 In conversation with K. Ohannessian (2011), 'Leadership Hall of Fame: Stephen R. Covey, Author of *The 7 Habits of Highly Effective People*', *Enablers of Greatness*, 18 February, available from: <http://enablersofgreatness.blogspot.ie/2011_02_01_archive.html> (accessed 29 January 2014).

Chapter 5

34 Juska, J. (2004), *A Round-Heeled Woman: My Late-Life Adventures in Sex and Romance*, London: Chatto & Windus/Random House.

35 Zilbergeld, B. (1999), *The New Male Sexuality: The Truth About Men, Sex, and Pleasure*, revised edition, New York: Bantam.

[36] Juska (2004, p. 21).
[37] Friday, N. (1973), *My Secret Garden: Women's Sexual Fantasies*, New York: Simon & Schuster.
[38] Foley, S.K., Kope, S. and Sugrue, D. (2002), *Sex Matters for Women: A Complete Guide to Taking Care of Your Sexual Self*, New York: Guilford Press.
[39] Administration on Ageing (2001), *A Profile of Older Americans: 2001*, Washington, DC: US Department of Health and Social Services.
[40] Central Statistics Office (2011), 'Census 2011 Results: Profile 2 Older and Younger – An Age Profile of Ireland', available from: <http://www.cso.ie/en/newsandevents/pressreleases/2012pressreleases/pressreleasecensus2011profile2-olderand younger> (accessed 8 September 2013).

Chapter 6

[41] Eugenides, J. (2011), *The Marriage Plot: A Novel*, New York: Farrar, Straus and Giroux, p. 93.
[42] Eugenides (2011, p. 160).
[43] Psalm 46:10.
[44] Williamson, M. (1992), *A Return to Love: Reflections on the Principles of a Course in Miracles*, New York: HarperCollins, p. 190.
[45] Lemon, B. (2012), *Retirement: A Memoir and Guide*, CreateSpace Independent Publishing Platform.
[46] Upson, S. (2012), 'Healthy Skepticism: Are Believers really Happier than Atheists?', *Scientific American*, 23(2), pp. 59–63.
[47] Upson (2012, p. 59).
[48] Upson (2012, p. 59).
[49] Davis, A. (2013), 'Dealing with Religious and Spiritual Issues in "Secular" Psychotherapy: From the Perspective of Clients and Therapists', PhD thesis, Trinity College Dublin, p. 10.
[50] Davis (2013, p. 14).
[51] Upson (2012).
[52] Upson (2012, p. 63).
[53] Ruskin, J. (2012), *Modern Painters Vol. III. Containing Part IV., of many things*, Project Gutenberg EBook #38923, available from: <http://www.gutenberg.org/files/38923/38923-h/38923-h.htm> (accessed 29 January 2014).
[54] Megarry, B. (2013), 'Facing Up to the Truth About Life Before Death', *Irish Times*, 29 January, pp. 12–13.

55 Neustatter, A. (2013), 'Coming of Age', *Psychologies Magazine*, pp. 85–87, p. 87.

Chapter 7

56 Gibran, K. (1926), *The Prophet*, London: Fakenham and Reading, p. 20.
57 O'Morain, P. (2012), 'Accepting Our Humble Lot Can Be Good for Us', *Irish Times*, 31 July, p. 14.
58 Joseph, J. (1992), 'Warning', *Selected Poems*, Tarset: Bloodaxe.
59 In conversation with the author, June 2013.

Bibliography

Acevedo, B. and Aron, A. (2009), 'Does a Long-Term Relationship Kill Romantic Love?', *Review of General Psychology*, 13(1), pp. 59–68.

Administration on Ageing (2001), *A Profile of Older Americans: 2001*, Washington, DC: US Department of Health and Social Services.

Alton, B. (2011), *Retirement: An Opportunity to Upgrade Your Health*, Retirement Planning Course, Dublin: Civil Service Training and Development Centre, 113–114.

Brickman, D., Coates, D. and Janoff-Bulman, R. (1978), 'Lottery Winners and Accident Victims: Is Happiness Relative?', *Journal of Personality and Social Psychology*, 36(8), pp. 917–927.

Buettner, D. (2004), *Blue Zone: Lessons for Living Longer from the People Who've Lived the Longest*, New York: National Geographic.

Centre for Clinical Interventions (nd), 'Mindfulness and Letting Go', *Centre for Clinical Interventions*, available from: <http://www.cci.health.wa.gov.au/docs/ACF3C6F.pdf> (accessed 31 August 2013).

Central Statistics Office (2011), 'Census 2011 Results: Profile 2 Older and Younger – An Age Profile of Ireland', available from: <http://www.cso.ie/en/newsandevents/pressreleases/2012pressreleases/pressreleasecensus2011profile2-olderandyounger> (accessed 8 September 2013).

Clark-Flory, T. (2011), 'How Common Is Infidelity, Anyway?', *Salon*, 12 June, available from: <http://www.salon.

com/2011/06/12/infidelity_3/> (accessed 3 March 2013).

Covey, S.R. (1989), *The 7 Habits of Highly Effective People: Powerful Lessons in Personal Change*, New York: Simon and Schuster.

Covey, S.R. (nd), 'The 90/10 Principle', *Office of Medical Student Affairs, Indiana University*, available from: <http:// msa.medicine.iu.edu/files/2713/3236/9537/90-10 Principle.pdf> (accessed 8 September 2013).

Curtin, J.S. (2002), 'Living Longer, Divorcing Later: The Japanese Silver Divorce Phenomenon', *Global Communications Platform: The Japanese Institute of Global Communications*, available from: <http://www.glocom. org/debates/20020805_curtin_living/> (accessed 20 September 2013).

Davis, A. (2013), 'Dealing with Religious and Spiritual Issues in "Secular" Psychotherapy: From the Perspective of Clients and Therapists', PhD thesis, Trinity College Dublin.

Erikson, E.H. (1959), *Identity and the Life Cycle*, New York: International Universitites Press.

Eugenides, J. (2011), *The Marriage Plot: A Novel*, New York: Farrar, Straus and Giroux.

Foley, S.K., Kope, S. and Sugrue, D. (2002), *Sex Matters for Women: A Complete Guide to Taking Care of Your Sexual Self*, New York: Guilford Press.

Friday, N. (1973), *My Secret Garden: Women's Sexual Fantasies*, New York: Simon & Schuster.

Gaffney, M. (2007), 'The Pursuit of Happiness', *Irish Times*, 25 August, pp. 18–19.

Gaffney, M. (2011), *Flourishing*, Dublin: Penguin Ireland.

Gallacher, D. and Gallacher, J. (2011), 'Are Relationships Good for Your Health?', *Student British Journal of Medicine*, available from: <http://student.bmj.com/student/ view-article.html?id=sbmj.d404> (accessed 28 January 2014).

Gibran, K. (1926), *The Prophet*, London: Fakenham and Reading.

Gottman, J. (1994), *What Predicts Divorce? The Relationship Between Marital Processes and Marital Incomes*, Hillsdale, NJ: Lawrence Erlbaum Associates.

Gottman, J. (1998), 'Psychology and the Study of Marital Processes', *Annual Review of Psychology*, 49, pp. 169–197.

Greer, C. (2013), 'What Are You Thinking? (Part Deux)', *Charlie Greer's HVAC Profit Booster*, available from: <http://www.hvacprofitboosters.com/Tips/Tip_Archive/tip_archive7.html> (accessed 28 January 2014).

Handy, C. (2012), 'Relationships Ireland – Keynote Speech', Relationships Ireland 50th Anniversary Conference, June, Dublin.

Holmquist, K. (2007) 'Digging Deep', *Irish Times*, Weekend Section, 25 August.

Joseph, J. (1992), 'Warning', *Selected Poems*, Tarset: Bloodaxe.

Juska, J. (2004), *A Round-Heeled Woman: My Late-Life Adventures in Sex and Romance*, London: Chatto & Windus/Random House.

Lemon, B. (2012), *Retirement: A Memoir and Guide*, CreateSpace Independent Publishing Platform.

Magee, A. (2008), 'A Happy Balance', *Red Magazine*, July, pp. 229–232.

Marshall, A. (2010), *How Can I Ever Trust You Again? Infidelity: From Discovery to Recovery in Seven Steps*, London: Bloomsbury Publishing.

Megarry, B. (2013), 'Facing Up to the Truth About Life Before Death', *Irish Times*, 29 January, pp. 12–13.

Murray, J.G., Murray, J.D., Swanson, C.C., Tyson, R. and Swanson, K.R. (2002), *The Mathematics of Marriage: Dynamic Nonlinear Models*, Cambridge, MA: MIT Press.

Murray, M. (2009), 'Realising the True Value of Your Life', *Irish Times*, 21 April, p. 11.

Neustatter, A. (2013), 'Coming of Age', *Psychologies Magazine*, pp. 85–87.

Newman, M. (2007), *Emotional Capitalists: The New Leaders*, Chichester: John Wiley & Sons Ltd.

Ohannessian, K. (2011), 'Leadership Hall of Fame: Stephen R. Covey, Author of *The 7 Habits of Highly Effective People*', *Enablers of Greatness*, 18 February, available from: <http://enablersofgreatness.blogspot.ie/2011_02_01_archive.html> (accessed 29 January 2014).

O'Morain, P. (2012), 'Accepting Our Humble Lot Can Be Good for Us', *Irish Times*, 31 July, p. 14.

Power, C.D. (2012), 'Field of Dreams', Speech delivered at graduation ceremony, John Scottus School, 24 May, Dublin.

Ruskin, J. (2012), *Modern Painters Vol. III. Containing Part IV., of many things*, Project Gutenberg EBook #38923, available from: <http://www.gutenberg.org/files/38923/38923-h/38923-h.htm> (accessed 29 January 2014).

Scheibehenne, B.M., Matta, J. and Todd, P.M. (2011), 'Older But Not Wiser: Predicting a Partner's Preferences Gets Worse With Age', *Journal of Consumer Psychology*, 21(2), pp. 184–191.

Sigle-Rushton, W. (2010), 'Men's Unpaid Work and Divorce: Reassessing Specialization and Trade in British Families', *Feminist Economics*, 16(2), pp. 1–26.

TILDA (2011), *Fifty Plus in Ireland 2011: First Results from the Irish Longitudinal Study on Ageing*, Dublin: Trinity College Dublin.

Upson, S. (2012), 'Healthy Skepticism: Are Believers really Happier than Atheists?', *Scientific American*, 23(2), pp. 59–63.

Wehrenberg, M. and Coppersmith, L. (2008), 'Technotrap: When Work Becomes Your Second Home', *Psychotherapy Networker*, pp. 40–45 and 64.

Williamson, M. (1992), *A Return to Love: Reflections on the Principles of a Course in Miracles*, New York: HarperCollins.

Zilbergeld, B. (1999), *The New Male Sexuality: The Truth About Men, Sex, and Pleasure*, revised edition, New York: Bantam.

Suggested Further Reading

Mindfulness

Anthony de Mello, *Awareness* (Image Publishing/Random House, 1990).

Paul Gilbert, *The Compassionate Mind* (Constable, 2009).

Jon Kabat-Zinn, *Full Catastrophe Living: Using the Wisdom of Your Body and Mind to Face Stress, Pain and Illness* (Piatkus, 1990).

Jon Kabat-Zinn, *Wherever You Go, There You Are: Mindfulness Meditation in Everyday Life* (Piatkus, 1994).

Jon Kabat-Zinn, *Coming to Our Senses: Healing Ourselves and the World through Mindfulness* (Piatkus, 2005).

Chris Mace, *Mindfulness and Mental Health: Therapy, Theory and Science* (Routledge, 2008).

Thich Nhat Hanh, *Peace Is Every Step: The Path of Mindfulness in Everyday Life* (Rider & Co., 1995).

Eckhart Tolle, *The Power of Now: A Guide to Spiritual Enlightenment* (Namaste Publishing, 1997).

Mark Williams and Danny Penman, *Mindfulness: A Practical Guide to Finding Peace in a Frantic World* (Piatkus, 2011).

Sexuality

Jennifer Berman and Laura Berman, *For Women Only: A Revolutionary Guide to Overcoming Sexual Dysfunction and Reclaiming Your Sex Life* (Henry Holt, 2001).

Alain de Botton, *How to Think More about Sex* (Pan Macmillan, 2012).

Sallie Foley, Sally A. Kope and Dennis P. Sugrue, *Sex Matters for Women: A Complete Guide to Taking Care of Your Sexual Self* (Guilford Press, 2002).

Nancy Friday, *My Secret Garden: Women's Sexual Fantasies* (Simon & Schuster, 1973).

Andrew G. Marshall, *How Can I Ever Trust You Again? Infidelity: From Discovery to Recovery in Seven Steps* (Bloomsbury, 2010).

Bernie Zilbergeld, *The New Male Sexuality: The Truth about Men, Sex, and Pleasure*, (Bantam, 1999).

Mental Health

Tony Bates, *Depression: The Common Sense Approach* (Gill & Macmillan, 1999).

David D. Burns, *The Feeling Good Handbook: Using the New Mood Therapy in Everyday Life* (William Morrow, 1989).

Maureen Gaffney, *Flourishing* (Penguin Ireland, 2011).

Helen Kennerley, *Overcoming Anxiety: A Self-Help Guide Using Cognitive Behavioral Techniques* (Robinson, 1997).

Don Miguel Ruiz, *The Four Agreements: A Practical Guide to Personal Wisdom* (Amber-Allen Publishing, 1997).

Áine Tubridy, *When Panic Attacks* (Gill & Macmillan, 2008).

Useful Resources

Retirement

Active Retirement Ireland
Stated purpose is to enable retired people to enjoy a full and active life and to advocate for them
124 The Capel Building, Mary's Abbey, Dublin 7
01 873 3836
info@activeirl.ie
www.activeirl.ie

American Association of Retired Persons
Provides a wealth of information aimed at retired persons
www.aarp.org

Irish Senior Citizens' Parliament
A representative, non-partisan political organisation working to promote the views of older people in policy development and decision-making
90 Fairview Strand, Dublin 3
01 856 1243
seniors@iol.ie
http://iscp.wordpress.com

My Aged Care
Information source for over 50s in Australia
www.myagedcare.gov.au

Older Women's Network (Ireland)
A national network linking individuals and groups of women
aged 55+
Senior House, All Hallows College, Grace Park Road, Dublin 9
01 884 4536
ownireland@eircom.net
www.ownireland.ie

The Retirement Planning Council of Ireland
Provides support, information and guidance to people planning for retirement
Pinebrook House, 72–74 Harcourt Street, Dublin 2
01 478 9471
information@rpc.ie
www.rpc.ie

Volunteer Ireland
The national volunteer development agency, which works to
promote and celebrate volunteering in Ireland
18 Eustace Street, Temple Bar, Dublin 2
01 636 9446
info@volunteer.ie
www.volunteer.ie

VSO Ireland
International organisation for volunteering abroad
Second Floor, 13–17 Dawson Street, Dublin 2
01 640 1060
info@vso.ie
www.vso.ie

Nutrition

Bord Bia
Aims to bring the taste of Irish food to more tables
Clanwilliam Court, Lower Mount Street, Dublin 2
01 668 5155

info@bordbia.ie
www.bordbia.ie

Drink Aware
Consumer information on alcohol consumption
01 611 481
info@drinkaware.ie
www.drinkaware.ie

Irish Nutrition and Dietetic Institute
Provides a list of accredited dieticians
Ashgrove House, Kill Avenue, Dun Laoghaire, Co. Dublin
01 280 4839
info@indi.ie
www.indi.ie

National Dairy Council
Educates consumers on the role of dairy in their lifestyles
Innovation House, 3 Arkle Road, Sandyford Industrial Estate, Dublin 18
01 290 2451
info@ndc.ie
www.ndc.ie

Safe Food
Promotes awareness and knowledge of food safety and nutrition issues on the island of Ireland
7 Eastgate Avenue, Eastgate, Little Island, Co. Cork
021 230 4100
Block B, Abbey Court, Lower Abbey Street, Dublin 1
01 448 0600
Helpline: 1850 404 567 (ROI), 0800 085 1683 (NI)
info@safefood.eu
www.safefood.eu

Health and Fitness

Ageing Well Network
An independent group of leaders, heads of organisations and strategic thinkers who share a vision of an Ireland that is one of the best countries in the world in which to grow old
16–17 College Green, Dublin 2
01 612 7040
info@ageingwellnetwork.ie
www.ageingwellnetwork.com

Alcoholics Anonymous
A fellowship of men and women who share their experience, strength and hope with each other in order to overcome their alcoholism and help others to recover from alcoholism
Unit 2, Block C, Santry Business Park, Swords Road, Dublin 9
01 842 0700
gso@alcoholicsanonymous.ie
www.alcoholicsanonymous.ie

Alzheimer Society of Ireland
A national voluntary organisation that aims to provide people with all forms of dementia, their families and carers with the necessary support to maximise their quality of life
National Office, Temple Road, Blackrock, Co. Dublin
01 284 6616
Helpline: 1800 341 341
info@alzheimer.ie
www.alzheimer.ie

Growing Stronger
Strength training programme for older adults
www.cdc.gov/nccdphp/dnpa/physical/growing_stronger

Health Finder
American government-run health information source
www.healthfinder.gov

Health Promotion Unit
HSE-run website that provides information on a wide range
of health issues
healthinfo@hse.ie
www.healthpromotion.ie

Irish Cancer Society
National charity providing support and information to those
affected by cancer, and supporting research into cancer
prevention and treatment
43/45 Northumberland Road, Dublin 4
01 231 0500
Lawley House, Monahan Road, Cork City
021 484 0597
Helpline: 1800 200 700
reception@irishcancer.ie
www.cancer.ie

Irish Heart Foundation
The national charity fighting heart disease and stroke
50 Ringsend Road, Dublin 4
01 668 5001
Helpline: 1890 432 787
www.irishheart.ie

Irish Osteoporosis Society
A charity dedicated to reducing the incidence of osteoporosis and promoting bone health
114 Pembroke Road, Garden Level, Ballsbridge, Dublin 4
01 637 5050
Lo-call: 1890 252 751
info@irishosteoporosis.ie
www.irishosteoporosis.ie

Medline Plus
American government-run medical information source
www.medlineplus.gov

Real Age
Personalised healthcare advice
www.realage.com

Mental Health

AWARE
A voluntary organisation that provides support group meetings for people with depression and manic depression and their families
72 Lower Lesson Street, Dublin 2
01 661 7211
Helpline: 1890 303 302
info@aware.ie
www.aware.ie

Bodywhys
Provides help, support and understanding for people with eating disorders, their families and friends
PO Box 105, Blackrock, Co. Dublin
01 283 4963
Helpline: 1890 200 444
info@bodywhys.ie
www.bodywhys.ie

GROW
GROW aims to help the individual grow towards personal maturity by using their own personal resources, through mutual help groups in a caring and sharing community
Grow National Office, Barrack Street, Kilkenny
056 776 1624
1890 474 474
info@grow.ie
www.grow.ie

Mental Health Ireland
A national voluntary organisation that aims to help those who are mentally ill and to promote positive attitudes to mental health
Mensana House, 6 Adelaide Street, Dun Laoghaire, Co. Dublin
01 284 1166
information@mentalhealthireland.ie
www.mentalhealthireland.ie

National Service Users Executive
Gives service users, family members and friends a voice in how their mental health services are planned, delivered, evaluated and monitored
085 121 2386
info@nsue.ie
www.nsue.ie

Out and About
The national organisation for sufferers of agoraphobia
140 St Lawrence's Road, Clontarf, Dublin 3
01 833 8252
www.nire.ie/index.asp?docID=365

Recovery International
A community mental health organisation that offers a self-help method of will training
Bridge House, Cherry Orchard Hospital, Ballyfermot, Dublin 13
01 626 0775
info@recovery-inc-ireland.ie
www.recovery-inc-ireland.ie

Samaritans
The primary aim of Samaritans is to be available at any hour of the day or night to listen to and befriend those experiencing personal crises and those in imminent danger of taking their own lives. All contact is in complete confidence

4–5 Usher's Court, 7 Usher's Quay, Dublin 8
01 671 0071
1850 609 090
jo@samaritans.org
www.samaritans.org

Shine – Supporting People Affected by Mental Ill Health
A national organisation dedicated to upholding the rights
and addressing the needs of all those affected by enduring
mental illness
38 Blessington Street, Dublin 7
01 860 1620
Helpline: 1890 621 631
info@shineonline.ie
www.shineonline.ie

Counselling, Psychotherapy and Mediation

Family Therapy Association of Ireland
For a list of registered individual, couple and family therapists
73 Quinn's Road, Shankill, Co. Dublin
01 272 2105
www.familytherapyireland.com

Irish Association of Counselling and Psychotherapy
For a list of counsellors and psychotherapists in Ireland
21 Dublin Road, Bray, Co. Wicklow
01 272 3427
Locall: 1890 907 265
iacp@iacp.ie
www.irish-counselling.ie

Irish Council for Psychotherapy
For a list of all registered psychotherapists in Ireland
13 Farnogue Park, Wexford
01 902 3819
www.psychotherapy-ireland.com

Mediators' Institute of Ireland
For a list of accredited mediators
Pavilion House, 31/32 Fitzwilliam Square South, Dublin 2
01 609 9190
info@themii.ie
www.themii.ie

Mindfulness

Center for Mindfulness in Medicine, Health Care, and Society
Provides a number of mindfulness tools and programmes
University of Massachusetts Medical School, Boston, United States
+1 508 856 2656
mindfulness@umassmed.edu
www.umassmed.edu/cfm

Centre for Mindfulness Research and Practice
Provides training in mindfulness-based approaches to healthcare
Centre for Mindfulness Research and Practice, School of Psychology, Dean St Building, Bangor University, Bangor, LL57 1UT, Wales
+44 (0)1 248 382498
mindfulness@bangor.ac.uk
www.bangor.ac.uk/mindfulness

Mindfulness.ie
General information on mindfulness courses
info@mindfulness.ie
www.mindfulness.ie

Mindfulness Ireland
Mindfulness courses and details
info@mindfulnessireland.org
www.mindfulnessireland.org

Oscailt
Provides regular mindfulness courses
8 Pembroke Road, Dublin 4
01 660 3872
info@oscailt.com
www.oscailt.com

Oxford Cognitive Therapy Centre
Provides an online shop to purchase books and CDs cover-
ing all the practices used in Oxford's Mindfulness-Based
Cognitive Therapy programme by Mark Williams
Warneford Hospital, Oxford, OX3 7JX, England
+44 (0)1 865 738816
octc@oxfordhealth.nhs.uk
www.octc.co.uk

PadraigOMorain.com
A short guide to mindfulness
www.padraigomorain.com/the-quite-short-guide-to-mind
fulness.html

The Sanctuary
Provides regular mindfulness courses
Stanhope Street, Dublin 7
01 670 5419
enquiries@sanctuary.ie
www.sanctuary.ie

Organisations for Carers

Care Alliance Ireland
Provides information and support to family carers
Coleraine House, Coleraine Street, Dublin 7
01 874 7776 / 087 207 3265
info@carealliance.ie
www.carealliance.ie

The Carers' Association
National voluntary organisation for and of family carers in the home
Bolger House, Patrick Street, Tullamore, Co. Offaly
057 932 2920 / 057 932 2664
Careline: 1800 240 724
nationalcareline@carersireland.com / info@carersireland.com
www.carersireland.com

Caring for Carers Ireland
Voluntary support organisation for carers
2 Carmody Street Business Park, Ennis, Co. Clare
065 686 6515
support@caringforcarers.org
www.caringforcarers.ie

HSE Support for Carers
Information and support from the HSE for carers
National Information Line: 1850 24 1850
www.hse.ie/eng/services/list/4/olderpeople/carersrelatives/Support_for_Carers.html

Pensions

Irish Association of Pension Funds
Provides representation and other services for those involved in operating, investing and advising on all aspects of pensions and other retirement provision
Suite 2, Slane House, 25 Lower Mount Street, Dublin 2
01 661 2427
info@iapf.ie
www.iapf.ie

Office of the Pensions Ombudsman
Investigates and decides complaints and disputes from individuals about their occupational pension schemes, Personal Retirement Savings Accounts (PRSAs) and Trust RACs
36 Upper Mount Street, Dublin 2
01 647 1650
info@pensionsombudsman.ie
www.pensionsombudsman.ie

Useful Contacts for the Elderly

Age Action Ireland
A charity which promotes positive ageing and better policies and services for older people
30/31 Lower Camden Street, Dublin 2
01 475 6989
info@ageaction.ie
www.ageaction.ie

Age NI
Delivers care services, provides advice and advocacy, fundraises and influences decision makers in Northern Ireland to improve later life for all
3 Lower Crescent, Belfast, BT7 1NR
+44 (0)28 9024 5729
Advice Helpline: 0808 808 7575
info@ageni.org
www.ageuk.org.uk/northern-ireland

Age and Opportunity (Ireland)
A national organisation that inspires everyone to reach their full potential as they age; it aims to turn the period from age 50 onwards into one of the most satisfying times in people's lives, by facilitating opportunities in arts and culture, sport and physical activity, learning and active citizenship
Marino Institute of Education, Griffith Avenue, Dublin 9
01 805 7709

info@ageandopportunity.ie
www.ageandopportunity.ie

ALONE
Supports older people in need through a befriending service, long-term housing and crisis support in the community
Olympic House, Pleasants Street, Dublin 8
01 679 1032
enquiries@alone.ie
www.alone.ie

Carelocal
Non-profit organisation which works to alleviate loneliness and isolation in Dublin's older community
Crosscare, Clonliffe College, Dublin 3
01 836 0011
carelocal@crosscare.ie
www.carelocal.ie

Friends of the Elderly
A volunteer-based Irish charity that alleviates social isolation and loneliness amongst older people through friendship
25 Bolton Street, Dublin 1
01 873 1855
info@friendsoftheelderly.ie
www.friendsoftheelderly.ie

Senior Helpline
Confidential listening service for older people by trained older volunteers for the price of a local call anywhere in Ireland
C/o Third Age, Summerhill, Co. Meath
LoCall: 1850 440 444
info@thirdageireland.ie_
www.thirdageireland.ie/what-we-do/14/senior-helpline/

Bereavement

Bethany Bereavement Support Group
A voluntary parish-based ministry which aims to help the bereaved and grieving
Rathfarnham Parish Centre, Willbrook Road, Rathfarnham, Dublin 14
087 990 5299
bethanysupport@eircom.net
www.bethany.ie

Console
National organisation supporting people in suicidal crisis and those bereaved by suicide
Console House, 4 Whitethorn Grove, Celbridge, Co. Kildare
01 610 2638
National Helpline: 1800 201 890
info@console.ie
www.console.ie

Recreation

Contract Bridge Association in Ireland
The official regulator for the recognised game of contract duplicate bridge in Ireland
Templeogue House, Templeogue Road, Dublin 6W
01 492 9666
www.cbai.ie

One Foot Abroad
Walking and adventure holidays
16/17 Suffolk Street, Dublin 2
01 443 3973
info@onefootabroad.com
www.onefootabroad.ie

General

Citizens Information
Provides information, advice and advocacy on a broad range of public and social services
0761 07 9000
www.citizensinformation.ie

Consumers' Association of Ireland
Protects, promotes and represents the interests of Irish consumers
26 Upper Pembroke Street, Dublin 2
01 637 3961
cai@thecai.ie
www.thecai.ie

Crime Victims Helpline
Offers confidential support and information to victims of crime in Ireland
Freephone: 116 006
Text: 085 133 7711
info@crimevictimshelpline.ie
www.crimevictimshelpline.ie

Department of Health
Government department which formulates and evaluates policies for the health services
Hawkins House, Hawkins Street, Dublin 2
01 635 4000
www.doh.ie

Department of Social Protection
Government department which provides a wide range of social and community supports and services
Áras Mhic Dhiarmada, Store Street, Dublin 1
01 704 3000
www.welfare.ie

Disability Information Ireland
Provides support and information for those with a disability
in Ireland
01 505 9435
info@disability.ie
www.disability.ie

Energy Action Ltd
Charity which provides free home insulation in order to alleviate fuel poverty in Dublin
IDA Unit 14, Newmarket, Dublin 8
01 454 5464
connect@energyaction.ie
www.energyaction.ie

European Anti-Poverty Network Ireland
A network of groups and individuals working against poverty
in Ireland
Equity House, Upper Ormond Quay, Dublin 7
01 874 5737
info@eapn.ie
www.eapn.ie

Family Diversity Initiative
A coalition of organisations working with and representing
the interests of diverse families in Ireland. This coalition
recognises that the family exists in many different structures and circumstances
c/o One Family, Cherish House, 2 Lower Pembroke Street,
Dublin 2
info@familydiversity.ie
www.familydiversity.ie

Financial Regulator
Part of the Central Bank; regulates financial services and institutions in Ireland
Consumer Information Department, Financial Regulator, P.O. Box 9138, College Green, Dublin 2
1890 777777
enquiries@centralbank.ie.
www.centralbank.ie/regulation/Pages/home.aspx

Health Service Executive
Provides all of Ireland's public health services, in hospitals and communities across the country
Oak House, Millennium Park, Naas, Co. Kildare
045 880 400
Dr Steevens' Hospital, Dublin 8
01 635 2000
infoline1@hse.ie
www.hse.ie